£4-95

9c9u

THE BRITISH MUSEUM
Purpose and politics

THE BRITISH MUSEUM

Purpose and politics

David M. Wilson

PUBLISHED FOR THE TRUSTEES OF THE BRITISH MUSEUM
BY BRITISH MUSEUM PUBLICATIONS

© 1989 The Trustees of the British Museum

Published by British Museum Publications Ltd
46 Bloomsbury Street
London WC1B 3QQ

British Library Cataloguing in Publications Data

Wilson, David M. (David Mackenzie), *1931*–
    The British Museum: purpose and politics.
    1. London. Camden. (London Borough). Museums:
    British Museum
    I. Title
    069'.09421'42

ISBN 0-7141-1714-5

Designed by Jenny Chattington

Typeset in Palatino by Rowland Phototypesetting Ltd
Bury St Edmunds, Suffolk
Printed in Great Britain by
Richard Clay Ltd, Bungay, Suffolk

CONTENTS

PREFACE

This book stems from impatience. Despite every endeavour through the media, political debate and public statement, it has proved impossible to place before the public the complicated practicalities of running the British Museum, and the philosophy upon which it was founded. I here attempt to present a balanced picture of a great institution which lives in the world but struggles to make itself understood. It is aimed at informing politicians and the media as well as the general public, who are clearly interested in everything that happens in museums. It is also an appeal for help and sympathy. Some of the detail is technical, but I have tried to provide a clear picture of the Museum's hopes, beliefs and problems. The problems are largely political, using the term in the widest possible sense – hence the title of the book. The opinions expressed are my own but do, I trust, reflect the ideas and aspirations of the Trustees and of my colleagues. (They will soon tell me if they do not!)

The book has been written in two months, and written on the hoof – in airport lounges in Japan, Jordan and America, on trains and in aircraft, in hotel bedrooms, in excavation houses, and at home during weekends. It was drafted quickly with the idea of providing an impression of the Museum and its problems in 1989; time is short and our problems urgent. I could not have written it without the active support of the Trustees and the staff of the Museum (many of whom have provided me with information), the encouragement of British Museum Publications Ltd and the patience of my wife.

I would particularly thank, for their advice and help, Jean Rankine (the Deputy Director of the Museum) for relieving me of many administrative burdens and Marjorie Caygill (my Assistant) for checking the figures. They, with Graham C. Greene, one of the Museum's Trustees, read this book in draft and saved me from much error of fact and emphasis. Dorothy Mitchell, Andrea Hill, Jane Nixon and Joyce Brammall typed it, puzzling out my minute handwriting and enthusiastic ballooning with skill and patience. Jenny Chattington saved the book by skilful editing.

I am also grateful to colleagues at home and abroad, too numerous to mention, who have been sympathetic listeners and advisers. Without their generosity with their time I could not have completed this work.

DAVID M. WILSON
JUNE 1989

INTRODUCTION

The image of the British Museum as a dusty, dull, ill-lit institution, full of decaying mummies and marbles, its basements
replete with neglected treasures and its café full of curly-edged
sandwiches, lingers in the mind of many as an easy, dismissive
cliché. Journalists from the quality press insultingly label the staff
'gloomy troglodytes'. Vocal and unthinking groups call for the
return of objects to their country of origin and equally vocal
groups demand the return of the Front Hall to its 'original' colour
scheme. The 'arts lobby' calls for us to spend millions of pounds
which we do not have on Old Master drawings; archaeologists
accuse us of élitism, and the government, whilst steadily reduc-
ing financial support for museums, tells us not to whinge. Some
advise us to become more commercial; others berate us for
succumbing to the pressures of big business. We are accused of
being patronising to indigenous peoples of the Third World and
to people who do not live in London. Many say, 'charge for entry
and solve all your problems'. It is said that we do not know what
we have; that we have too much and that we are interested in
acquisition only for its own sake.

The Museum is not without its faults or its problems, some of
them self-engendered. But the Museum is a vibrant and exciting
institution; it pulsates with life, and is attractive to casual visitors
and scholars alike. Some four million visitors pass through its
doors every year. It has public support of a deeply rooted kind:
London taxi-drivers, American academics, Japanese tourists,
French school-children, Hong Kong businessmen, British
auction-houses, Russian professors, Inuit hunters and a whole
kaleidoscope of nationalities and interests are affected by us, help
us, seek knowledge from us or simply enjoy us. The British
Museum entertains and instructs, curates and conserves. Its staff

– which numbers more than a thousand – includes architects and designers, warders, curators, craftsmen, accountants and a host of trades and professions. Between them they speak over fifty languages and read more than sixty. They attend to world experts in Umayyad inscriptions and answer questions about grandmother's teapot. They teach Chinese art, are consulted by Nigerian museum curators, give conservation advice to small countries in the Pacific and lend major exhibitions to Australia. The Museum's publications company produces more than thirty books each year and the restaurant provides us with 20 per cent of its takings as payment for a licence to operate. We are host to ballets, concerts, lectures, conferences and business conventions. We deal with the press and provide packs for teachers. We welcome heads of government on official visits. We run a successful shop and provide free exhibitions to museums throughout the country. Our auditors and staff inspectors provide a national service in their own professional fields; we host meetings of many professional bodies. We raise money in Japan and the United States and excavate in Iraq and Italy.

These are but some of the varied and exciting activities of the British Museum. Those who unthinkingly attack us generally do so out of ignorance; a few people just do not like us. This book aims at righting misconceptions and answering criticisms. It is intended to show how the Museum functions; it is avowedly a pamphlet to stimulate discussion. The facts given here are as far as possible just that: they are accurate. The opinions are based on discussion, planning and experience, both within the Museum and outside it. This book presents a view of the Museum and its functions as seen from the centre; it cannot always portray it in the pastel colours of individual endeavour and opinion at ground level, but it can, I hope, provide something more than a black-and-white snapshot of current Museum thought at all levels.

The impression given might sometimes be defensive, for in some ways (mainly financial) we feel embattled and need to appeal for public and political sympathy. At the same time I hope to express a positive attitude to collections, public, government and the academic community. It is intended to show that we are not rudderless and inefficient, rather that we work to a plan and perform numerous services for the national and international community. If I appear to complain it is not to 'whinge'; it is to point to inequities which could with goodwill be righted by public, individuals or government. The main purpose of this book is to dispel widespread ignorance about a great national and international institution.

It is also written on behalf of all national museums and galleries in Britain, few of whom do not feel underfunded and neglected. The climate of governmental opinion seems to be turned against established institutions; an overworked sponsor department struggles to understand and help but it is under pressure elsewhere with problems, for example, in the performing arts. The museum problem is here to stay and must be recognised. Most of my colleagues in the other leading national museums in this country would and could plead similar cases. The problems outlined here do not only affect this country, they are of enormous interest abroad. In many ways, Britain leads the museum profession: what affects us often has implications elsewhere. Wherever I have travelled during the course of the last six months I have been met with anxious enquiries about, and genuine concern for, the health of the museum system in the United Kingdom. This explains the title of the book: the British Museum lives in the world and is subject to all sorts of political pressures, has a major diplomatic role and is the subject of great concern both in this country and abroad. This book is a plea for understanding and help.

Chapter 1
'THAT NOBLE CABINET'

The British Museum was founded in 1753 by Act of Parliament to house the collections bequeathed to the Nation by Sir Hans Sloane. It has been funded by Parliament since that date, and the main tenets of the original British Museum Act and its various successors have formed a model and a basis for the legislation which has governed the other national museums in the United Kingdom. Parliament and the Nation approved the Museum's foundation and have supported it as a major national asset ever since. It was the first public, corporate museum in the world and it is now arguably the greatest.

The Museum is a product of its age. The universalist theories of Diderot and the Encyclopaedists shaped its function and the ideas of its founder. In its collections was material illustrating the sum of human knowledge. Sloane was a physician, a naturalist and an antiquarian; his acquaintances were widespread – Voltaire, Handel, Franklin, Queen Anne and the whole gamut of eighteenth-century academe. His collections included, for example, Chinese paintings, West Indian botany, native American artefacts, medieval manuscripts, stuffed alligators, drawings by Dürer, Renaissance medals and thousands of books. The whole of man's knowledge of man was framed in his vast collections. Sloane's vision encompassed a universal collecting policy; his philosophical view of material culture and nature formulated the policy of the Museum, of the institutions which sprang from it, the British Library and the British Museum (Natural History), for all time.

Sloane's bequest posed a problem for Parliament, which was initially reluctant to raise money to house the collection, and to provide the £20,000 for Sloane's daughters required in his will. Led by Speaker Onslow, however, an Act was passed founding the Museum; provision was made for a lottery to fund its housing and a board of Trustees was established to protect the collections and the institution from public or parliamentary whim. A grand house – Montagu House in Great Russell Street – was bought, and in 1759 the Museum opened its doors for business. The doors were only opened a crack, but certain important principles were established at the outset which have remained with the Museum ever since: first, the collections should be held in perpetuity in their entirety; second, the collections should be freely available to the curious; third, the Museum should be curated by full-time specialists. The trustees of Sloane's will became the core of the Trustees of the British Museum, together with representatives of the families who had assembled the two great libraries of Cotton and Harley which were added to the Sloane bequest. The collections consisted of antiquities, natural history and printed books and manuscripts. Natural history moved to the British Museum (Natural History) in South Kensington in the 1880s and in 1996 the British Library will move to St Pancras, both these bodies being made independent of the British Museum Trustees by Acts of Parliament of 1963 and 1972. Under the 1963 Act the constitution of the Board of Trustees was altered to include one member appointed by the Sovereign, fifteen appointed by the Prime Minister, five appointed by the Trustees themselves, and one each appointed on the nomination of the Royal Society, the British Academy, the Royal Academy and the Society of Antiquaries of London. In most other respects the 1963 Act reflects and enshrines the original 1753 legislation.

The Museum attracted gifts from the year of its opening. The first major acquisition of classical antiquities, for example, was given by Thomas Hollis in 1757. The Museum was in effect a part patron of Captain Cook's Pacific voyages, particularly through Sir Joseph Banks (later a powerful Trustee); in 1772 we acquired the first of Sir William Hamilton's two collections of Greek vases, and in 1802 the Rosetta Stone and other Egyptian antiquities came to Bloomsbury as a result of the British military expedition to Egypt (these became Crown property under the Treaty of Alexandria and were presented to the Museum by George III). The first major purchase, although it was really a deal, was the Townley collection of classical sculpture from Italy, made by means of a Parliamentary grant of £20,000 in 1805. With the foundation of a

Department of Antiquities two years later a more professional and rigorous acquisition policy was initiated. A major loan was the Portland Vase (purchased more than a century later from the then Duke of Portland). The Bassae Frieze and the Elgin Marbles came in 1815 and 1816 respectively, and important Egyptian sculptures (acquired by Henry Salt and Giovanni Belzoni) were purchased somewhat reluctantly in 1823. In 1825 the Payne Knight bequest of books, bronzes, coins and drawings gave a considerable academic boost to the collections. Rich's collections from Mesopotamia introduced a new element to the Museum in 1825, and in the following year the appointment of a polymathic Keeper of Antiquities, Edward Hawkins, set the Museum on an active collecting path which has continued to the present day.

By this time Montagu House was wearing out; it had never been intended as a museum, and the Nation decided that something worthy should be built to house what was rapidly becoming one of the greatest collections in the world. The first and grandest element, the King's Library (built to house the library of George III), was completed in 1827; it is one of the most splendid rooms in London, and its future use has to be carefully considered in the Museum's plans following the removal of the British Library in 1996. The main Museum building, of which the library formed a wing, was designed by Sir Robert Smirke at a cost to the Nation of £800,000 and was completed in 1852. The building of the Museum continued in an almost unbroken progression until 1914. First came the construction of the great circular Reading Room between 1854 and 1857, with the consequent destruction of the fine classical courtyard and the 1877 extension of the entrance hall. In 1880 the Natural History collections began their move to South Kensington and the vacated galleries were filled with antiquities from such newly founded Departments as the Department of British and Mediaeval Antiquities and Ethnography. Between 1880 and 1884 a new wing was built on the site of the Principal Librarian's garden on the Montague Street front with funds bequeathed by William White; shortly afterwards the Trustees, with the authority of an Act of Parliament of 1894, began to buy up the freehold of the houses on all sides of the Museum with the intention of building a vast extension which would clothe the whole building with an additional series of magnificent galleries. The first phase was the only one completed – the Edward VII

Building on the north side of the Museum – which was opened in 1914. Although it was recognised early in this century that the Museum needed new buildings, government money has built only one minor extension since 1914, the 'New Wing' opened in 1979 to house small special exhibitions and a substantial part of the administrative staff. A private gift provided the Duveen Gallery, which was built to house the Parthenon sculptures; this was completed in 1939, bombed during the Second World War and not finally opened until 1962. An impressive extension for Japanese antiquities is to be opened in 1990, paid for entirely from private donations, mainly from Japan.

One consequence of the lack of major publicly funded development in the last seventy years has been the need to move parts of the collections from the main building. In Burlington Gardens, behind Piccadilly, a building originally constructed as the Senate House of London University and now known as the Museum of Mankind became the home of exhibitions of the Department of Ethnography. Storage for reserve collections has been provided at two sites, one in Shoreditch and the other near Olympia. Unfortunately, the Trustees own the freehold of the latter only – the other buildings are leased – but this problem will disappear with the opportunity to move most of the exiled departments and material back to Bloomsbury in 1996 when the British Library moves.

The pressure on space has always been a problem for the Museum, and it has been the trigger for all the major building projects. The shortage of space is due partly to the massive expansion of the collections. Edward Hawkins in the active forty years of his keepership of the Department of Antiquities was encouraged to build up the collections of the Museum. Prints and Drawings became a separate department in 1836, but the rest remained under his control until 1860. Hawkins was a tyrant, but he encouraged acquisition and scholarship, the latter particularly evident in his appointment of a number of assistants in his Department, especially of a young man of twenty-five who became an Assistant in 1851 – Augustus Wollaston Franks. Franks was wealthy, had polymathic interests and the imagination to indulge them. He was socially gregarious and, with his solid upper middle class background, had the entrée to all the important houses and collections. He was a considerable scholar, an innovative prehistorian and one of the greatest connoisseurs of his generation. He it was who, almost alone, created the non-classical and Near Eastern collections of the Museum after he had become head of the newly created Department of British and Mediaeval Antiquities in 1866. He purchased widely out of his own pocket, he persuaded the government to do deals, he exchanged material with other collectors, and he encouraged benefactions and bequests of material to the Museum. The Slade collection of glass; the Christy collection, which is the core of the Department of Ethnography; the Bridge collection of Indian sculpture and the Bernal collection of medieval and Renaissance objects: these are but some of the varied materials he steered toward the Museum. He himself gave the Museum collections of prehistoric artefacts, medals, fifty-two thousand book-plates, pottery and porcelain, silver plate, medieval armour and Japanese ceramics, as well as finger-rings and knick-knacks beyond number. By the time he retired in 1896, knighted and full of honours, he had increased the Museum's collections immeasurably; he attempted to convey his achievement in a memorandum written just before his death:

> When I was appointed to the Museum in 1851 the scanty collections out of which the department has grown occupied a length of 154 feet of wall cases, and 3 or 4 table cases. The collections now occupy 2250 feet in length of wall cases, 90 table cases and 31 upright cases, to say nothing of the numerous objects placed over the cases or on walls.

Franks' work was paralleled elsewhere, and the Keepers of the other departments – Coins and Medals, Prints and Drawings, Oriental (i.e. Egyptian and Assyrian) and Greek and Roman Antiquities – built the collections assiduously. This was not done idly, for the sake of collecting. The scholars who worked in the Museum were extending human knowledge through the study of material culture: not art historians, they were the first professional archaeologists and ethnographers. They published widely both inside the Museum and outside. It was from this time that the words *British Museum Catalogue* on a publication proclaimed unequalled scholarship in material culture – a reputation which continues to this day.

The expansion of the antiquities collections, which in effect started about 150 years ago, was in the first instance almost accidental, but whereas most museums of the period were basically curiosity cabinets, at the British Museum a great deal of effort was put into the academic study of the collections, and this led eventually to the establishment of acquisition policies. Sometimes such policies were rather grand: the expeditions of Rawlinson and Layard to Mesopotamia which brought back the great Assyrian sculptures, for example, and Fellows' work at Xanthos, which resulted in the acquisition of the great classical Greek monuments (the Nereid Tomb and its companion pieces). These and similar excavations were enormous undertakings which could only be achieved with considerable official help from the Royal Navy, Royal Engineers and other official arms of government. More typical were the early attempts to collect archaeological material. The Roach Smith collection chiefly of Romano-British antiquities found in London during the early nineteenth century stimulated the remarkable growth in collecting objects from the British and European pre- and protohistoric periods which helped promote the general understanding of the European past. Franks was in close touch with scholars in Copenhagen and Mainz who were developing the discipline of prehistoric archaeology and was himself the first scholar to isolate and examine Celtic art. He was also responsible for the Museum's acquisition of the Continental material from the great Iron Age sites at Hallstatt and La Tène; interestingly, he also wrote about and collected Japanese prehistoric material. Excavations were at that time largely privately funded, and the generosity of landowners and amateur excavators brought some of the material found into the Museum.

In the field of coins – and later of medals – the British Museum soon achieved pre-eminence. The first catalogue (of the Museum's holdings of Greek coins) was published in 1814, and both Hawkins and his predecessor Taylor Combe wrote standard works on numismatics in the second quarter of the nineteenth century. Prints and Drawings had split from the Department of Printed Books as early as 1808, when it became a subdivision of the Department of Antiquities, and apart from the disastrous failure in 1838 (due to public indifference and lack of government funding) to buy the great Lawrence collection of drawings, the Museum rapidly acquired the core of the national collection in this area.

The growth of the collections was matched by an increase in the number of visitors, putting further pressure on the building. When it was founded, and until well on into the nineteenth century, the Museum was, theoretically at least, open to everyone. Visitors applied for a ticket (which was complicated to obtain) and were shown round at a rather breathless pace in parties of five or ten by a member of staff (a practice which ceased in 1810). It was not only the *bon ton* who came to the Museum; as early as 1784 the Trustees noted (perhaps rather disapprovingly) that visitors 'consisted chiefly of Mechanics and persons of the lower Classes'. It was presumably the need to satisfy the curiosity of these people, together with the need to attract the middle classes and provide a more scientific service, that Parliament began to take an interest in the subject on the grounds given by one MP that 'the public paid for the Museum and therefore had a right to insist on every facility of ingress'. After a Parliamentary Select Committee examined the problems of the Museum in 1835 and 1836 the government grant was raised and visitors were encouraged to come to the Museum – even those of the lower classes who might otherwise be 'besotting themselves in public houses'. On Easter Monday 1837 the Museum opened on a public holiday for the first time and 23,895 visitors were recorded (120 per day had been considered rather too much in 1810). This number was not exceeded until well into this century, although the visitors in 1851 (the year of the Great Exhibition) numbered more than a million. At this time a 'synopsis' of the Museum was produced for the visitor. It cost one or two shillings. The first general guide was produced in 1761, describing the general contents of 'that Noble Cabinet', and similar aids to the visitor have been produced ever since; today they range from a free pamphlet to a highly illustrated colour book.

The growth in the number of visitors was a major element leading to the construction of the new building, but it should be noted that when the Smirke building was finally opened only 300,000 visitors were catered for each year. The hall was slightly enlarged in 1877, but neither Smirke nor the Trustees of the time had any idea that by the 1980s four million or so visitors would each year have to be filtered through a very inadequate and non-elastic entrance before they could see a single object.

The security of the collections and the supervision of the visitors is, therefore, a major problem. Sight lines for warders generally preclude an intimate, and therefore unsupervisable, mode of display, so much of the collection has to be displayed under glass or behind barriers. The enjoyment, study and appreciation of the collections on public display remains, however, one of the prime functions of the Museum.

It is for this reason that great attention is given to display. The demands of modern exhibition techniques and the increasing sophistication of the audience combine with the problems of space, offering further challenges in using an old building to its best advantage. Early illustrations and descriptions give an impression of a rather secretive approach to the objects. Visitors were expected to come in awe, to wonder and not to ask too many questions. The collections were sometimes displayed in crowded conditions, with some attempt at order but little at elucidation. Some effort was made to please the eye, and surviving illustrations of the Townley Gallery (the first but rather short-lived specially built suite of rooms in the Museum), show a balanced display and tempting vistas, much in keeping with the classical taste of the Regency. Even the stuffed giraffes and rhinoceros placed at the head of the grand staircase of Montagu House were at least in scale with the building and did not look altogether incongruous (although the taxidermy apparently left something to be desired). We know little about labelling at this period, but presumably it was minimal and information was passed on by word of mouth.

The new building was, of course, purpose-built as a museum. Within the limits of the expertise of the time, attention was paid by the architect to security, to the scale of the objects, and to their visibility. Gas and candles were ruled out as too dangerous a source of light, and no provision was made for evening or winter use of the Museum. When it got dark, the Museum simply closed. Wall-cases were installed to Smirke's original design (some of these have been preserved in a gallery recently rearranged to display the exhibition 'The Greeks in Southern Italy'). Smirke's cases became the basic model for all show-cases built until 1914. Table-cases of various design were added as the collections expanded, and some of these survive today (for example, in room 33, the main Oriental gallery).

As new acquisitions were made and further examples added to the display, so the density of the exhibitions increased. Photographs surviving from the turn of this century show the crowded cases which typify the idea of a museum to many older visitors, and even after the Second World War there was a tendancy to perpetuate this style of display. Designers were not consulted; the curators dressed their own cases and some at least typed their own labels. Labels on free-standing sculpture were hand-lettered (the Museum has a splendid tradition in this area), as were some of those for the more important objects (a number of these can still be seen in the unreformed upper galleries).

Over the years different styles of exhibition, changing taste and unthinking additions led to hideous *ad hoc*-ery. By the early 1970s plaster-board partitions hid the architecture; the insides of cases were painted with coarse distemper; and the labels were, to put it kindly, enigmatic. Only in one or two important instances were any information panels introduced into the display. Compared with the primary galleries at the Victoria and Albert Museum, which had been carefully remodelled after the Second World War under the direction of Sir Leigh Ashton, the British Museum was a mess.

Two things changed this. First, the gradual repair of the considerable bomb damage suffered by the Museum enabled the Duveen Gallery, containing the Parthenon Frieze, to be opened. This gave rise between the mid-1960s and 1981 to the complete refurbishment of the sculpture galleries on the ground floor under the direction of outside designers. The appointment of a full-time designer in 1964 to advise the keepers on the display of their collections marked the first step towards the establishment of a design department which, after an epic battle with the Property Services Agency in 1979, now has sole charge of all the design in the Museum. The work of this section is described in chapter 5: here it should merely be stated that design plays an immensely important role, and has transformed the displays in three-quarters of the Museum from a mish-mash of diverse objects into well-labelled and coherently explained exhibitions. Not only are the objects shown to greater advantage, but they are also kept in conditions agreed with conservation officers, who work alongside designers and curators to bring the cultures of the world before an audience which has increased more than fourfold since 1960.

Much has changed in almost a century and a half since Smirke's museum was opened to the public. The redesign of the galleries in a style more sympathetic to the modern museum visitor has been a major priority in the last twenty years. And improvements in the galleries have been matched by the improved state of the buildings themselves. In the mid-1970s the external condition of the Museum and its general services were ruinous: the acres of roof leaked and bins of sawdust were kept in each gallery to catch dripping water. The drains – not having been serviced for years – were blocked and heavy rain often resulted in flash-floods in storage areas. The electricity supply was inadequate and the areas behind the scenes looked tawdry and untidy. By agreement with our sponsor department, the Office of Arts and Libraries, we foreswore all bids for new buildings in order to spend money on repair and maintenance. Symbolic of this was the cleaning and repair of the great Smirke façade. The grime of more than a hundred years was carefully removed, the stonework was repaired at vast expense and the great railings which were beginning to rust were stripped and repainted. A rolling programme of roof repair was started, and the sawdust disappeared from the public galleries. The drains were cleaned and, where necessary, renewed. By the end of 1990 a new ring-main and three new electricity sub-stations will have been installed (rewiring will follow). A programme of cleaning store-rooms and removing the muck of ages from the basements is now well in hand.

Until recently a charge of exclusivity and disapproval of visitors was still raised from time to time against the Museum, perhaps best remembered in the popular cautionary tale *The boy who breathed on the glass in the British Museum* by H. M. Bateman, published in 1916. But today the Museum, once forbidding and unhelpfully arranged, is brighter, cheerful and welcoming.

Chapter 2

COLLECTING

Central to the whole idea of a museum are the collections. The curator's first duty is to care for them, to keep them safe and to see that they do not deteriorate. After these priorities the curator has a duty to make the collections available to the public, either through display or publication, or by freely allowing the scholar or the interested public to study them in detail. These priorities are – or should be – common ground to all museum professionals. In order to make the collections easily available each object must be identified, recorded and labelled, and the curators must know where the individual items are. They must survey the collections constantly and get to know all the items in their charge.

The British Museum differs from other museums only in scale. The whole staff of the Museum – a complement of some 1130 people – is devoted to the ends outlined above. Only some 200 of the Museum's workforce are curators; there are also 70 conservation officers and 26 natural scientists, who investigate the technology and age of the objects in the Museum's care. There are ten curatorial departments which by their expertise cover (however thinly at times) the material culture of most of the world. The titles of the antiquities departments signify in general terms the areas covered: Japanese, Oriental, Greek and Roman, Western Asiatic (i.e. the ancient Near East), Egyptian, Prehistoric and Romano-British, [European] Medieval and Later, and Ethnography (i.e. the material culture of indigenous peoples). Two departments – Prints and Drawings, and Coins and Medals – deal with discrete types of objects, but non-European prints, drawings and paintings are kept in the appropriate antiquities department.

Most of the curatorial staff are academics, but some more junior members of the curatorial staff fulfil more technical roles: mounting objects for exhibitions, moving antiquities about the Museum or packing them in preparation for travel. The Museum is proud of the academic status of its curators, a status which is firmly founded on a thorough knowledge of its collections. Through publication and participation in academic discussion, by lecturing and teaching and by means of excavation and field-work, they are fully integrated into the scholarly life of this and many other countries. The list of British and foreign academies, universities, research institutes and academic committees in which members of staff participate is long and honourable. The collections depend on the scholarship and continuing experience of the staff, without which the Museum would be a junk-yard of curiosities, assembled without thought or order.

The process of collecting and the management of collections already in the Museum are complicated. Policy, accident and serendipity all play their part in the process of collecting and, as the collections grow so their management grows more labour-intensive, more expensive. In most museums there is an assumption that no parts of the collections can be disposed of: in the British Museum this assumption is backed by Act of Parliament. The 1963 Act only allows us to dispose of duplicates; objects which under certain provisions are 'unfit to be retained in the collections of the Museum and can be disposed of without detriment to the interests of students'; or objects which have 'become useless for the purposes of the Museum by reason of damage, physical deterioration, or infestation by destructive organisms'.

The assumption that the collections should, save in special circumstances, remain at all times in the Museum is founded on pragmatic grounds. Experience has shown that if objects are 'de-accessioned' their disposal is frequently regretted. Some museums and galleries have sorry tales to tell. Consider, for example, a picture by Fantin-Latour sold from the Lady Lever Gallery (now part of the National Museums and Galleries on Merseyside) in 1958. The picture was sold for £9,045. When it next appeared on the market the Museum considered its repurchase, but its selling price of £950,000 was well beyond the means of even a major publicly funded institution. It was for this reason that in the late 1960s under the wise advice of a senior English lawyer, Lord Radcliffe, sometime Chairman of the Trustees of the

Museum, a definition of the word 'duplicate' was hammered out, this remains the basis of the Trustees' interpretation of this clause in the Act to this day. In effect, duplicates are objects struck from the same die or printed from the same block or plate.

Disposal is a matter which has been much discussed in Parliament and the press in recent years. This discussion is the result of an accident. A relatively harmless clause introduced into a portmanteau parliamentary bill, which was intended to tidy up certain anomalies in museum and heritage legislation, included a section on disposal similar to that enshrined in the British Museum Act. In the event the bill ran out of parliamentary time, but the press had a field day urging de-accessioning in vast areas of the collections – an idea never envisaged in the bill. Here it should be said that the Museum is not a factory with raw material passing in at one end and a finished product coming out at the other; neither is it a dustbin full of rubbish which should properly be junked, nor a treasure house to be dipped into when funds run low. The collections of the British Museum are held in trust for the Nation for all time, and they have been so held for nearly 250 years. The Museum's reputation rests upon its collections, the care taken of them and their availability to scholar and public alike. They are not to be disposed of at the whim of fashion or through public pressure. That is why the Museum has a Board of Trustees, a body which protects it from such forces. Disposal is nearly always a mistake.

The policy of non-disposal does, however, carry its own responsibilities. An acquisition policy has to be drawn up and the implications, financial and otherwise, of such a policy must be considered. Every acquisition must be carefully weighed and discussed. It is, however, useless to withdraw from the fray and decide not to collect (although we are sometimes urged to do so). A museum which does not collect is a dead museum, as can be seen in rather too many small independent museums, where the waning enthusiasm or death of the founder, or simply lack of funds, results in a neglected collection which casts a burden on the public purse or on the temper of the professionals who have to remedy the situation. The British Museum constantly reviews its acquisition policy, and in effect every item acquired by the Museum is approved by the Director and Trustees. (Although the Trustees may sometimes have been slightly surprised by the result: in the 1950s, to spare the blushes of the Board, it was decided that the acquisition of the earliest surviving British condom should appear before the Board as 'a piece of eighteenth-century armour' – such circumlocutions are rare.)

Acquisitions are not always planned. One of the more serious problems in this area for the Museum, for example, concerns the law of Treasure Trove. The Museum has a statutory position regarding this medieval institution, which is not unique to this country. The rights to objects of precious metal found in the soil was one of the regalities claimed by the Crown from the early Middle Ages. A Director of the British Museum, Sir George Hill, wrote the standard work on the subject in 1936. Basically, the law dictates that any object or group of objects of precious metal buried in the ground *animus revertendi* (i.e. with the intention that the owner should return to claim it/them) and for which no owner or heir can be identified may be claimed by the Crown. Most frequently such finds consist of coins (the hidden private wealth of an individual, for example, who may have come to a sticky end and consequently been unable to retrieve it). Anyone finding treasure of precious metal in the soil must report it to the police, the British Museum or other appropriate authority (or, in Wales and Northern Ireland, to the equivalent institution; the law is slightly different in Scotland). In England a coroner's jury enquires into the case and decides whether the find can be declared as Treasure Trove, a) because it is precious metal and b) because it was buried *animus revertendi*. Some bizarre judgements are occasionally reached by this method, but on the whole the system works. If a find is not declared Treasure Trove it is usually returned to the finder, landowner or owner forthwith. Such a case was the Sutton Hoo treasure, which was excavated in 1939. As a grave deposited with the intention that the objects should not be recovered but should accompany the deceased to a future life, it was declared by the coroner not to be Treasure Trove. The public spirit of the landowner, Mrs Pretty, in presenting the finds she thus acquired to the Museum is one of the most generous gestures we have received this century.

If the objects in a find are declared Treasure Trove and the finder has acted within the law, some of the more arcane practices of English double-think come into operation, designed to ensure that finds of artistic or historical significance find their way into museums, where they will be available for public inspection, and at the same time to provide an adequate reward for the finder. The arrangement is perhaps somewhat ramshackle and it depends on honesty and goodwill.

The British Museum will have studied the find. If it judges that it should be retained by a museum it will present a valuation to the Treasure Trove Reviewing Committee, an independent body set up by the Treasury to advise Ministers on the value of Treasure Trove. When this valuation is accepted it becomes the price which museums must pay if they wish to receive the Treasure Trove. The British Museum has first choice of objects found in England and woe betide the Museum if it has no cash at this juncture, for it either loses the find or is accused in the press of mean delay. The money is then paid on without deductions by the Treasury to the finder as his reward (unless the finder did not report the find fully and promptly or, for example, attempted to hide or dispose of it privately; in these cases rewards may be reduced or not paid at all). Finds which are not retained by museums are returned to the finders, who are free to dispose of them as they think fit. Even though the British Museum may have contributed months of the time of its staff spent identifying and cleaning finds, this cost is not reimbursed.

Another type of unplanned acquisition comes by bequest. Usually the potential donor will have discussed the bequest with the appropriate curator, who will have signified that the Museum is willing to accept it. But it occasionally happens that the Museum knows nothing of the bequest until the executor's letter arrives. Most bequests are acceptable, but the Museum has on occasion declined to take a legacy which was outside the scope of the collections or to which unacceptable conditions were attached.

Generally, however, we acquire within a collecting policy. This consists of something more than simple guide-lines, but allows for flexibility and is laid down by the Trustees on the basis of submissions by the curatorial staff. Every five years a committee largely made up of curators under the chairmanship of the Director compiles a Museum-wide policy. This is up-dated in the annual reports submitted by each department to the Trustees. Behind the policy lie certain unmistakable principles. For example, the Museum never knowingly acquires any object where there is any doubt concerning the legality of title. Objects of foreign origin are only acquired if the laws of the country of origin allow it, a point cleared as a matter of routine in any report submitted to the Trustees on a purchase or gift. The object must be worthy of the Museum primarily by reason of its academic importance and its historical value (this latter point is of great importance, for dated objects in the British Museum form a sort of vernier scale for similar objects elsewhere). Some few objects are acquired because they are stunningly beautiful, but aesthetic considerations rarely form a major element in a decision to acquire.

The Museum must also be able to afford to buy an object. This is not such an obvious principle as would appear from the plain statement. If we were to purchase items which would immoderately deplete our limited purchase funds, we would regret it with every opportunity subsequently missed. Thus, for example, we can no longer from our own resources afford to purchase major Old Master drawings. A single Raphael could cost more than the grant of £1.4m which we receive annually from the government. When with the assistance of the National Heritage Memorial Fund we bid £5.25m for a group of drawings from the Chatsworth collection, we were at the limit of the available money – we could go no further – although many, speaking with hindsight, could not appreciate this fact when the drawings fetched more than £20 million at auction.

Finally, we must remember that we collect beyond the confines of 'the national heritage'. The British Museum is not a museum of British antiquities. The Museum does of course have a responsibility for the collection of objects and works of art produced in this country, but this must not lead it along narrow insular lines of acquisition. The Museum collects for the whole world and forms a heritage which is not chauvinistic.

How then do we formulate our acquisitions policy? Two main phrases are used and misused throughout the museum: 'gap-filling' and 'extending the collections'. Both are meaningful and both describe a process, but both are open to abuse. By the first phrase we mean the active seeking for material which will fill a gap in our collections and by so doing enlarge our understanding of a subject and make the collection more logical. Thus, for example, we excavate in many parts of the world to find minor material in its archaeological context which will illuminate the understanding of comparative (and usually grander) pieces collected before modern scientific excavation techniques were developed. Such an example is the excavation of Iron Age graves in East Yorkshire; this has not only provided us with many new finds, but has enabled us to set in context and reinterpret similar rich material grubbed up haphazardly in the nineteenth century. Generous division of finds in many Near Eastern countries has also provided us with background material to many of the prestigious objects brought back to this country by adventurous archaeologists with little scientific training in the last century. An example of this is provided by the Museum's excavations in the Jordan Valley at an enormous mound known as Tell es-Sa'idiyeh. The rich finds from the cemetery, as well as the architectural details of the buildings found at the top of the mound, tell of a hitherto unexpectedly close Egyptian contact (perhaps even of political control) in the thirteenth and fourteenth centuries BC. The Jordanian Antiquities Service have been most generous in the *partage* they have allowed us over the last few years, giving us material hitherto unrepresented in our collections in exchange for our expertise and the other finds from the site.

Gap-filling also means, for example, the acquisition of artists' work of a kind unrepresented in our collections, work displaying new techniques, thoughts or images. It means buying coins to supplement our vast collections – a new mint, a new king, a new moneyer recorded on a coin will add to one of the most important numismatic collections in the world.

But the Museum cannot collect only in its well-worn tracks. It must extend its collecting into new areas and into new periods. For instance, the Museum possesses one of the most comprehensive collections of Japanese prints in the world; indeed, we have even sent a whole exhibition of Ukiyoe prints to Tokyo itself. A few years ago, however, it was realised that our collections stopped – with a few exceptions – somewhere about 1930. It was therefore decided to extend the collection by acquiring prints of more recent date. Two great collections (the Vergez and Petit) were purchased in the nick of time before prices rocketed. As a result the Museum's collections for the period 1930–1970 now rival others, even in Japan. To this was added by gift some eighty prints largely produced between 1982 and 1985 which, after being shown in the Museum, were presented to us by the College Women's Association of Japan. A similar aggressive policy has been pursued in the acquisition of modern prints, drawings and medals from the Western world. Some of these have startled the British public when they were exhibited (modern American prints, German Expressionist prints and modern Czech prints, for example). Other such collections are now being built up and the public will be impressed by the strength of our modern British drawing collection when it is displayed in 1991.

Some years ago the Museum decided to extend its collection of paper money. The few banknotes in our collection had lain undisturbed for many years. Enquiry showed that few, if any, working collections of this important material existed. An aggressive campaign to acquire by purchase, gift and loan soon provided us with an unparalleled collection: we were particularly pleased by the international response to an appeal to banks and national issuing authorities for specimens. The result of this campaign was a major exhibition and catalogue entitled *As Good as Gold*, which was mounted in association with the Bank of England in 1987. Here we were not collecting for collecting's sake: our concerns included the history of the banknote, the economic use and meaning of paper money, the method of design and manufacture, the use of money as propaganda and the history of security engraving and printing.

A fundamental policy decision concerned our ethnographic collections. For many years the Museum had acquired large collections and fine pieces either by gift, private treaty or purchase in the salerooms. Very occasionally specialists from the Museum would travel and collect. In the late 1970s the emphasis of our collecting policy shifted. This was partly because the big collections, formed largely by missionaries and colonial servants, ceased to come forward, as the functionaries of Empire died off. Then the rapid advance of Westernisation in many Third World countries meant that traditional crafts and products were dying out. It was decided, therefore, that, before a sea of plastic swept over the remaining indigenous societies, the Museum should generally eschew the purchase of prestige ethnographic items in the Western salerooms and turn instead to collecting in the field. Such collections would be made both by members of our own staff and by trained anthropologists from other institutions. For the price of little more than travel and shipping we have thus been acquiring carefully documented collections of indigenous technology and traditional crafts from areas as far apart as Guinea Bissau, the Sudan, Gujarat, Papua New Guinea, Mexico and a host of other countries. We have also invited craftsmen from these countries to work in the Museum of Mankind, demonstrating their skills and producing for us, for example, an Indonesian Toraja rice barn of Baruppa' type, a full-sized totem pole (now at the Horniman Museum in South London), and wooden and bone objects of Inuit origin.

Most of these collections have been put together with the active co-operation of the local museum authorities (and in most cases this co-operation has enriched the collections and experiences of the museums in our host countries as well). Many of the expeditions have led to exhibitions which have broken new ground in technique and experience, as witness the Asante exhibition, where the reconstruction of the nineteenth-century palace at Kumasi brought gasps of delight from British and Ghanaian alike. The number of expatriate visitors from the Indian sub-continent to the exhibition entitled *Vasna: Inside an Indian Village*, both in London and in Leicester (to which it was loaned), showed that immigrant communities also appreciate that we are presenting to second-generation immigrants some idea of the appearance of a land they may never see.

The Museum has always been interested in the influence of one culture on another and has in the past rather casually collected objects produced through the interaction of European and indigenous cultures. A remarkable example of such a collection was that formed in the nineteenth century of argillite sculptured souvenirs made by the Haida Indians of British Columbia. We now collect – sparingly – what is loosely termed 'airport art': objects made for tourists by traditional methods but adapted by the craftsmen to the taste, as they conceive it, of European or American purchasers. This may sound frivolous, but it is a real expression of the contact between cultures and demonstrates how a commercial approach affects traditional values – a worthy subject for comment at a time of racial tension and economic contact. More interesting, perhaps, is the Museum's acquisition of acrylic paintings from Australia, which demonstrate the lively continuity of the aboriginal sand-painting into a new medium.

These paintings were carefully purchased before prices rocketed in the late 1980s and, like airport art, reflect the interface between genuine indigenous tradition and the hard world of commercialism in which artists today live.

Although the Museum has now practically ceased buying the grand pieces of ethnographic art, an occasional gesture is made in this direction, as witness the purchase of a number of items of Melanesian origin from the George Brown collection, which were refused an export licence when Newcastle University sold them to Japan. In this case the Museum co-operated in the purchase with the Sainsbury Centre of the University of East Anglia and a number of other museums to save at least some of the finer artefacts collected by a missionary collector at the end of the last century and entrusted by him to a museum which was forced by its funding body to get rid of them.

The British Museum does, therefore, clearly recognise that we must occasionally buy prestige items in order to save major pieces of the national heritage.

Buying such objects often distorts our budgeting, because they can be very expensive. Thus we paid £1,275,000 for the solid gold font, commissioned in 1797–8 by the third Duke of Portland (1738–1809, twice Prime Minister) from the great English gold-smith, Paul Storr. We were only able to acquire this magnificient object through the generosity of an institution which has become a major benefactor, the National Heritage Memorial Fund. This fund (the National Land Fund) was set up in 1946 as a memorial to those who died in the two World Wars. After being pillaged by the Treasury at a moment of national financial crisis, the fund was reactivated under its present title in 1980 by an Act of Parliament introduced by the then Minister for the Arts and the Secretary of State for the Environment. Since that date it has spent some £100 million on items of national importance. Among the wide variety of things saved by the direct intervention of the Fund are great houses like Kedleston Hall in Derbyshire, rare flowers, medals, piers, scientific collections, films (*Blithe Spirit* for example), liter-ary manuscripts, and many works of art. The British Museum has rarely appealed to them in vain, although we appeal sparingly. It was only with the support of the National Heritage Memorial Fund that we were able even to approach the price asked in our abortive attempt to buy the Chatsworth drawings in 1984.

One of the most remarkable items purchased with the aid of the Fund was a watercolour, *The halt in the desert* by Richard Dadd, which was identified by experts on the popular television programme, 'The Antiques Road Show', to which it was taken by the owners from their garage. Another watercolour was Samuel Palmer's hauntingly beautiful *A cornfield by moonlight with the evening star*, which was also purchased with the aid of a grant from the Fund, as well as with grants from a number of other sources. This acquisition is interesting in that for the first time for many years the Museum tried to raise money for a purchase by national appeal. This entailed a great deal of hard work and although a fair number of people did contribute, less than £21,000 of the purchase price of £200,000 was raised in this way. We probably made a mistake in going to appeal in this case; a much more prestigious object of enormous national importance is the only kind of thing likely to move people's hearts on a scale large enough to make such an operation worthwhile. The Museum has not mounted such a major effort since 1933, when it purchased the Codex Sinaiticus from the Soviet government. The experience of other museums and galleries shows that appeals of this sort rarely raise large sums of money, but they are clearly useful in propaganda terms in that they raise public awareness of our problems.

One of the more important groups of material which the Museum tries to acquire consists of objects found in British soil which are crucial to the understanding of our past. In all cases we try to record the exact findspot, but the widespread use by amateurs of metal-detectors has flooded the market with items which have often lost their provenance. Where we are given access to such important objects we try to buy them. For this we are often criticised by lay purists, but the Trustees' public policy statement in this matter puts the problem in context:

> The British Museum deplores the deliberate removal of ancient artefacts from British soil other than by properly directed archaeological excavation, especially when the context of those artefacts is thereby left unrecorded and severely damaged. However, although the unauthorised excavation of such material from a scheduled monument is illegal and can never be condoned, much of what is discovered elsewhere is brought to light lawfully; persons in possession of it often have a legal title to dispose of it as they think fit. In these circumstances, the Museum has an

overriding duty to try to acquire such finds as it considers to be appropriate to the national collection. To refuse to follow this course would entail a serious loss to our heritage, since we would then lose the chance to see and record a great many objects. The Museum understands, and shares, the concern of the archaeological world, but since there is a ready market both here and abroad, the situation will not be remedied by a museum embargo. Selective acquisition remains, in our view, not only the practical, but also the proper course.

A recent find, presumably a votive offering to a temple, of miniature bronze shields (together with one or two items of riding equipment) which provides archaeologists with much new knowledge concerning the English Iron Age was purchased in 1989 for £80,000, with the aid of a 75 per cent grant from the National Heritage Memorial Fund. We are not always so lucky in capturing objects before they are smuggled out of the country, as witness one of the most remarkable hoards of very high-quality Roman bronzes of the second century AD from a Romano-British temple site at Icklingham, Suffolk – a scheduled ancient monument. It appears to have been found early in 1982 through the unauthorised use of a metal-detector. Photographs of sixteen objects, including bronze and silvered statuettes, heads and masks, came into the possession of the British Museum soon after they had left the country, but we could not immediately trace the objects; in 1988, however, the majority of them turned up at a dealer's showroom in New York. It was alleged that they had been brought out of England in the 1940s and had then been in a Swiss private collection (the number of Swiss private collections must be enormous!). The Getty Museum was interested in the finest piece, an inlaid bronze panther, and, suspecting that it was Romano-British, consulted the British Museum. Upon learning that it had been illegally excavated and illegally exported, the Getty Museum decided that it could not buy it, though we had encouraged them to do so in order that it should be available to scholars. It is thought that the panther, like other objects from the hoard, are now in a private collection in the USA.

In this instance we were able to co-operate with another museum – albeit abroad – to try to preserve the objects in the public domain. The co-operation was aborted, partially through uninformed media interference, and specialists consequently may not be able see the objects for many years to come. It should be said that while there may not be complete unanimity among my colleagues concerning the presence of British material in foreign collections, many of us feel that it is a good thing for our culture to be seen abroad, just as many countries are happy that some of their treasures should end up in the British Museum. Most British people feel a lifting of the spirit when they see a British item in a foreign museum – the Gainsboroughs in the Frick Collection in New York, a Lowry in the Setagaya Museum in Tokyo, Elizabethan silver in the Kremlin or a Turner in Philadelphia.

The *omnium gatherum* of the British Museum is the Department of Medieval and Later Antiquities, a department which covers all the material culture of Europe since the fourth century AD and of America since its Europeanisation, other than coins, medals, prints and drawings. Fortunately in some ways, considering their bulk, the Museum does not collect furniture and sculpture of Renaissance and later periods, which is left to the Victoria and Albert Museum by a compact which goes back to the middle of the last century, although our collections are enlivened, for example, by a Michelangelo torso, a Piranesi Vase, a remarkable series of Roubiliac sculptures (the latter purchased long before the V & A was founded), and a Barbara Hepworth sculpture. Neither do we collect paintings on canvas (our collections in this medium were distributed to other national bodies: to the newly founded National Gallery in 1824, and to the National Portrait Gallery by an Act of Parliament of 1878), nor illuminated manuscripts (now held in the British Library).

The Department of Medieval and Later Antiquities does collect excavated material, chiefly of the Migration and medieval periods. It has also collected in the field of industrial archaeology – the detritus of the eighteenth-century Longton Hall porcelain factory, for example, excavated by our own staff. It also collects applied arts of all periods. Carolingian ivories; Mosan enamels; medieval, eighteenth-century and Victorian tiles; clocks; reliquaries; gold plate; Huguenot silver; jewellery and objects relating to historical personages – these are but a few of the remarkable variety of items held. In some cases we appear to overlap with the Victoria and Albert Museum, but there is a difference. The Victoria and Albert Museum's main function is as the national museum of applied art and design; the British Museum is an international historical museum. Thus, for example, when we collect porcelain we attempt to assemble documented pieces, vessels or figures with dates or proper names painted on them. We also try to collect as many potters' marks – European and British – as possible in order to be able to identify the various factories. We collect items which represent significant technical advances in the development of the industry, and we try to cover all pottery from its origins to the present day. We do not collect great prestige pieces of fine craftsmanship, Berlin or St Petersburg vases for example; this is really the province of the Victoria and Albert Museum, as is studio pottery, like that of Lucy Rea or Bernard Leach. The result, as the 1984 Wedgwood exhibition demonstrated, is that we can usually display the history of a major factory, or – as was shown by the recent publication of *Documentary Continental Ceramics from the British Museum* – illustrate much of the history of the major European porcelain factories from our own collections. This approach continues to form the basis of the collecting policy of this section of the Department.

At a lowlier level but following similar principles, the same Department has collected for nearly twenty years what is known as the national reference collection of medieval pottery. This material, drawn from both British and European sites, makes it a place of pilgrimage for medieval archaeologists from all over Europe. Much of it consists of sherds willingly donated by excavators for the good of their subject. It is also one of the elements which is often misunderstood by critics of the Museum who refer to our 'cellars stuffed with treasures'. This is an academic archive of interest only to scholars.

This Department and the Department of Prehistoric and Romano-British Antiquities also hold considerable collections which are in fact the archives of excavations. These have been published by the excavators, but are needed for future reference by scholars as more facts come to light, new techniques are developed and new interpretations of the past are made. In a few cases the finds are from excavations conducted by the Museum, but we also act as a repository of last resort for material from excavations which have been conducted by the Historic Buildings and Monuments Commission and for which there is no easy place of storage near to the site of the dig. Much of this material is kept in a large store in Olympia in a building shared with the Victoria and Albert Museum and with the Science Museum. The cost of equipping the store of excavated material was covered by the Commission.

This great excavation archive has been assembled on behalf of the nation, as part of our heritage, and joins the large number of prehistoric and medieval collections acquired in the past (either by excavation or from casual finds) which form the basis of our knowledge of this country's unwritten history. It could be regarded as junk – indeed, much of it was thrown away by its original owners. But one example will suffice to illustrate the way in which new methods may allow scholars to draw more information from old material. A research project was begun nearly forty years ago on our vast collection of Neolithic stones axes, a popular form of archaeological curiosity and for many years little more than that. A nationwide petrological examination of these stones, which entailed the microscopic identification of the raw material, revealed the sources of the rocks used in their manufacture. Consequently scholars were able to identify axe factories in certain areas of the north and west of the British Isles. An examination of the distribution pattern of axes on the basis of the analysis showed that they were traded over long distances throughout Britain, thus providing one of the first pieces of evidence of a reasonably sophisticated trade nexus within the region.

In some areas it is now impossible for us to acquire, since to do so would contravene the law. The antiquities laws of the countries of the classical world – especially Greece, Italy, Turkey and Syria – are particularly draconian. Nothing can be exported legally from these countries, a situation which leads to a great deal of smuggling. The rigid interpretation of these laws can be demonstrated by one instance. At a symposium in Oxford in 1988 a paper was given on a coin-hoard of enormous importance smuggled out of Turkey into (ultimately) the United States; every scholar who attended has been banned by the Turkish authorities from ever again working professionally in that country, whether they had handled the coins or not. The British Museum did not touch a single coin from this hoard and would never have done so, but four of the Museum's staff were at the conference and have been so banned, although their only crime was to attend the lecture and discussion by some of the world's greatest experts on the hoard. This extraordinary decision strikes deeply at the base of academic freedom of expression, and we must wonder whether in these circumstances such a hoard can ever again be mentioned in academic publication.

But the Museum can still collect material from the classical world brought back to this country when it was legal to do so, particularly in the days when richer members of society travelled on the Grand Tour to Italy. Thus in the last few years the Museum has acquired a number of pieces of classical sculpture which have a long history in this country, including most recently two pieces given to us by the Residuary Body of the Greater London Council. Our collecting policy sees items from the Grand Tour collections as part of our heritage, in that they helped to form English neo-classical taste: it is for this reason that we continue to collect them.

But the most delightful and exciting part of collecting is serendipity: the sudden appearance, for example, of a long-lost antiquity or the recognition by one of our experts of a misattributed object. The unexpected arrival on our doorstep of a class of object which we had no idea existed (like the hoard of shields mentioned above) gives more thrill perhaps than any other single facet of the Museum's acquisition activity. In many cases we cannot plan acquisition: we can say that we wish to acquire classes of objects, French drawings of the late eighteenth and early nineteenth century, say; but we cannot go out and purchase a work by an individual artist, such as David, off the peg in a French dealer's showroom. Ultimately drawings of this date will be drawn to our attention, or will be found by our staff, and we will attempt to buy them or they will be given to us.

Some recent discoveries will illustrate various aspects of such happenstance. The example of the Richard Dadd painting has already been mentioned: for this we paid the market value it would have fetched in the salerooms. But even the auction houses are not always able to identify items correctly and by taking certain risks we have recently purchased through them an unrecognised Rembrandt drawing for £3,250 (bought at an Amsterdam auction and completely missed by all the Dutch specialists in this artist's work) and the bronze seal-die of Henry v when Prince of Wales as Lord of Carmarthen (which had been lost from sight since the eighteenth century) for just over £1,200. A drawing of Christ on the Cross bought in 1987 as 'attributed to Guido Reni' for £2,800 was a real bargain: the expertise of the Museum's staff was able to demonstrate that it is a finished study for the altarpiece by Reni of the Capucin Church outside Bologna (now in the Pinacoteca Nazionale in that city). Rarely, however, does a member of staff make a find quite so sensational as that made by a curator in the Prints and Drawings Department, who discovered a finished Gainsborough pencil landscape drawing in a Midlands second-hand shop and purchased it for £20. He gave it to the Museum.

Many people are happy to sell items to the Museum on very favourable terms. Just before his death in 1988 that most influential English print-maker Stanley William Hayter – a man who worked in Paris and New York and allowed many famous artists, including Picasso, to use his studio – was pleased to sell us the complete archive of his own prints which started in 1925 and continued until 1960. A similar archive of the work of David Bomberg at one of his most creative periods (between 1910 and 1919) was purchased from a friendly dealer, part of the purchase price being provided by the British Museum Society. (It should be said in parenthesis that the Museum never gives public valuations of objects. If we identify an object which we wish to buy we always send the potential vendor to an appropriate dealer or valuer, we never – with private buyers – make an offer.)

The importance of gifts of objects or collections to the Museum cannot be underestimated. Since the foundation of the Museum the British have been singularly generous in this fashion. A recent exhibition of the major donors to the Louvre was accompanied by a catalogue which listed all the benefactors of that great museum – nearly 2,700 in all. The British Museum probably has had a hundred times that number. Choosing two years at random (the calendar years 1985 and 1986), the Museum received a total of 107 major donations and 832 minor donations, many of which (in both classes) were multiple gifts. Legacies and donations range from the immense bequests of Franks and Christy to gifts of single items by modest collectors: we were particularly moved a few years ago by the gift of an early Turner watercolour of a Kentish scene by a lady who had persisted against advice in her belief that it had been painted by him – and was proved right!

Even the government gives us objects; we have, for example, a wide-ranging collection of official seal-dies given by the Colonial Office which represents all the individual colonies of old Empire. Sometimes gifts come with conditions attached: a skilful and eccentric lady, Mrs Anne Hull Grundy, gave the Museum an enormous collection of jewellery, mainly of the eighteenth, nineteenth and twentieth centuries, on condition that it should be permanently displayed and properly published. The condition of permanent display is one we rarely accept; possibly the only other such conditional gift was the bequest in 1898 by a former Trustee, the Baron Ferdinand de Rothschild, of the *objets de vertu* from Waddesdon Manor. In the case of the Hull Grundy gift it was clear that no such collection could be formed again and after much deliberation the Trustees accepted it – and the conditions which went with it. It is now one of our most popular displays and the great catalogue (published in record time) is an indispensable book for all historians of jewellery. This particular collection brought our collections of European jewellery up to date in one fell swoop. Perhaps the only thing missing from our jewellery collections are the very grand objects set with major stones – the parures of the great ladies of the eighteenth and nineteenth centuries. We are still looking for donors of such items, a rather ambitious area of expansion!

It is perhaps difficult for the general public to understand our collecting policy with regard to the other national museums, particularly the Victoria and Albert Museum and the Tate Gallery (but also the Science Museum and the various museums dealing with the armed forces). Generally, the British Museum collects material in an historical context; other museums have different collecting philosophies, the Victoria and Albert Museum, as we have seen, being particularly concerned with design. There is continuous discussion with the other national museums concerning our mutual collecting policies, so that there should not be too much overlapping or duplication; and we always make sure that we do not use taxpayers' money to bid against the purchase grant of other publicly funded institutions.

An example of such a potential clash of interest is the collection of twentieth-century works on paper which are acquired by the Tate Gallery and the British Museum. The British Museum acquires prints and drawings in areas not specifically covered by the

Tate, mainly for reference purposes in order to supply a context in which a given subject or artist can be studied; exhibitions provide a spur to collecting but do not form the reason for it. At the moment (apart from the Turner collections) the Tate Gallery has no plans for the development of full-scale study facilities for prints and drawings, but concentrates almost entirely on post-Second World War material, and particularly on the work of the last thirty years. The Tate records the development of contemporary European art as it is produced; the British Museum collects with the advantage of hindsight. Rarely do we challenge the other's expertise. The Tate will always rightly go for the impressive image, we for the context of the historically dated. The staff of the two institutions are in constant touch with each other and problems of conflict or duplication are usually worked out at a very early stage of any negotiations.

In all acquisitions the expertise, scholarship and experience of the academic staff of the Museum are of paramount importance. The daily contact with objects, whether already in the collections or brought in for opinions, builds up knowledge of periods, materials and cultures which become, or already are, the curator's own speciality. As junior members of staff, curators are set to cover areas well outside their own speciality in order to stretch their experience and to provide knowledge for the future. Every member of the Department of Coins and Medals, for example, deals on a rota basis with all coins brought in for identification. The Islamic specialist will ultimately, by consultation with specialists in other disciplines, become proficient in recognising the commonest type of coins, Roman or Chinese for example, submitted for identification by members of the public.

On my first day in the Museum as a very junior curator I was presented with three tasks; the one in my own speciality was the most difficult (to answer a query as to whether the Vikings ate onions), but I was also asked to identify a medieval wax plaque and find a particular eighteenth-century metal ticket associated with Handel which had been misplaced in the stores. Such is the training still practised to this day. A good museum curator is above all things curious about all objects, whether they be in his own subject or in some entirely different area. The museum curator proves his worth in the field, in the saleroom or in the dealer's showroom. He or she is trained to spot the important pieces. The curator who found the £20 Gainsborough is a specialist in Italian art of the Renaissance to the eighteenth century, but he is also a good museum man – a man with an eye.

Chapter 3
RECORDING AND CONSERVATION

A central duty of the museum curator is record-keeping: 'label it today, tomorrow you will have forgotten', are words inscribed on every curator's heart. Not only labelling, but the registration and the selective publication of the items in the collection are immediate obligations. Inventory and stock-taking have become matters of great public interest in the last few years, as a report of the National Audit Office drew attention to what it saw as serious deficiencies in the records of the British Museum and the Victoria and Albert Museum. In 1988 I defended the Museum against these criticisms before the Public Accounts Committee of Parliament and my defence was largely accepted by them. Journalists, however, had a field-day with their 'shock-horror' reports and a lot of mud, unjustifiably flung, still clings to our image. Recent events in other museums have reopened the controversy. It is proper that the Museum's methods of recording should be properly understood before criticisms are voiced.

The Museum has virtually complete inventories of its holdings, and a great deal of money and effort has been invested in compiling them. From the earliest days the Museum had handwritten 'registers', ledgers which listed objects acquired by the Museum by gift or purchase. By the late 1820s these registers had become formalised and a system of numeration developed which is still used today. A typical entry is illustrated in fig. 1. The number 1908,4–11,1 means that the object was the first item acquired on 11 April 1908. Such registration numbers are written on all objects in the collections (other than coins and medals), and one of the primary duties of every Assistant Keeper was and still is to register acquisitions as they are made. It is a boring job, but one that is taken very seriously, for the details of provenance, acquisition, material and size recorded in the register (often with

Date.	No.	Description.
4 — 11	1	Stoneware bottle, speckled-grey, brownish within, slight mouldings round the lip, otherwise plain, string marks on base. H. 3.8
4 — 13	1	Porcelain figure of a boy on ornamental plinth, right fore-arm missing, left hand raised & holding grapes, grapes on head, and basket of fruit on plinth beside left foot. H. 5.8″
4 — 14	1	Porcelain wine-pot, square with angular orifice at top and handle, spout curved and the whole covered with tortoiseshell glaze, characters in sepia on plain white base, in three rows. H. 3.9″
4 — 15	1	Pottery bowl, broken & repaired, reddish inside & outside below the neck which is convex & washed yellow with painted irregular fret in dark brown; slight foot rim chipped. D. 7.8″ H. 3.4″
	2	" bowl, yellow all over, with the neck painted in dark brown, in four panels, two patterns alternating; foot rim. D. 6.1″
	3	" bowl, similar to last but with heart-shaped leaves in panels. D. 6″
	4	" bowl, with broad flat lip ornamented with chevrons in brown paint, the body with alternate panels in brown. D. 5¾″
	5	" bowl, mended, thin ware, yellow with lozenges in brown, D. 4.7″ brown line inside lip, and foot rim on angular base.

Fig. 1. A register entry.

a thumb-nail sketch for ease of identification) are the foundation of all ensuing scholarship. A Roman spoon with no such identification is simply a Roman spoon; it might be interesting in itself, but it becomes much more interesting to the specialist if its find-place is known and any associated finds are recorded. Thus the spoon might be part of a hoard found with fourth-century coins and with other pieces of tableware at Canterbury, a major Roman town. It is on the basis of such evidence that the archaeologist may build a picture of life in the Roman Empire, of technology, of trade, of eating habits, of wealth, and so on. This information is important to scholarship; the register itself is important for housekeeping, for checking the collections, and for public audit and other non-academic purposes.

How acquired.	Pass.d	Bill.	Inc.d Cat.d	Observations.
...by D.r Horace Jeaffreson, Red House, Wandsworth.				About 1700, Fulham ware.
...given by J. Charbonnier, Esq. at Galleries, Lynmouth				Plymouth porcelain, of experimental appearance.
given by R. L. Hobson, Esq.				Inscription = 14.th day of 10.th month of 3.r.d year of Kayei (1850), made by Nü-no-gunjiro. Japanese.
given by J. H. Marshall, Esq. Director-general of Archaeology for India.				See Archaeological Survey of India, Annual Report, 1904-5, p. 105. Revue Archéologique, 1909, 156. From Hal (...) of Cal...(...)

It would be idle to pretend, however, that the older ledgers and card indexes provide a complete modern record function. If the description is inadequate or wrong the identification and location of the object can be difficult, especially as the continual creation and reforming of departments through the Museum's history has meant that objects in old inventories have migrated and are now scattered in different departments. A recognition by the Trustees that the records were not altogether satisfactory led in 1971 to a project intended to tidy up such muddles. Additional staff were hired on a temporary basis to search physically through the collections and to inventory objects that did not appear to be already registered. The Museum can state, therefore, with some confidence that a record exists for the whole of the collection, save only for items omitted through human error, or items which have been reserved for inventory through the computer project outlined below.

The major problem concerning the records lies in the lack in certain departments of an adequate location index. Location indexes of some objects are kept, but since such records were not created from the beginning, they are by no means universal. On the other hand, the curatorial staff's knowledge of the collections and their experience of handling them makes it virtually certain that an individual item can be quickly found. This fact is not easy for outsiders to understand. How, they say, can you identify, among the millions of objects held by the Museum, a single item? The easiest way of explaining this is to take the simplest example. A collector wishes to see a specific silver coin of Harun al-Rashid from the Samarqand mint. The curator instead of looking up a record goes to a labelled cabinet which contains in purpose-made drawers some 240 coins of that caliph, arranged by metal, mint and date. He opens the appropriate drawer and finds all the coins of the particular mint, locates the coin requested, makes a security record of the tray and takes it to the student. Not all antiquities, however, are little round things like coins, but the principle is the same. Prints – of which we have some two million – are kept in boxes or folders, under subject, artist or school, and are found in a similar fashion to that described for coins. Medieval belt-buckles or pottery, cuneiform tablets, Egyptian papyri, eighteenth-century finger-rings or Fijian spears are all found in the same way. The only hiccoughs occur when an object is misplaced through human error. Here only the expertise of the curator can retrieve the situation by recognising the missing piece. Sometimes this may take a considerable time. Fortunately such occurrences are rare, but however good the storage or complete the records this type of error is one of the most difficult to guard against in enormous collections like those of the British Museum. The stringency of routines developed for obvious security reasons renders it practically impossible to misplace coins, for they are guarded with an almost Dobermann-like ferocity; if a Fijian spear, however, is misplaced it might end up in an African rack. But as our systems get more sophisticated, such problems become less frequent.

The collections are consulted with great frequency; for

example, some six thousand students use the Prints and Drawings Students Room yearly. Consequently misplacements and losses and even thefts do occur, just as handling by students may risk damage to the objects. But in a system as open to scholarship and research as that run by the Museum such depredations are inevitable and, within the greatest possible security, must be accepted. No form of record-keeping can prevent accident or the determined or original theft.

A great deal of emphasis has been placed by our auditors on the computerisation of the collections. It is thought that this will provide more immediate and controlled management of the collections. To this task the Museum has added another function, that of providing an information retrieval system to aid research and maintain information about the collections. We hope that through this system we will be able to provide quick information about the collections and also that we shall be able finally to rebut the oft-repeated canard, 'they don't know what they've got.'

In fact, the Museum has been using computers in its scientific work since 1973. When required by the Public Accounts Committee in 1981 to provide a computerised record of the collections for stock-taking purposes we were not altogether without some expertise in these mysteries. We also knew that it would not be a simple or short process. A senior specialist had already been appointed in 1978 to complement the computer staff based in the Research Laboratory and he had by 1981 started to investigate the problem and construct a program. Existing systems for museum collections did at that time exist in theory. Some had been tried and failed; few had sufficient relevance to the British Museum's requirements, particularly in regard to scale. We looked at the very advanced system used by the National Air and Space Museum in Washington (developed for the cataloguing of aircraft images) and at the Canadian Heritage Information Network. We learnt from others' failures, which were many. Ultimately we implemented the United Kingdom's Museum Documentation Association's software package, GOS, and started cautiously to put our collections on record. It should be said in parenthesis that, although this obligation has been laid on us by Parliament and although our sponsor department, the Office of Arts and Libraries, did battle for us, we did not receive (so far as we can understand the intricacies of government funding) a single extra penny for this project. In fact, in order to finance it we have had to cut staff in other areas. We estimate that the total capital and development costs of producing the computerised inventory will be in the neighbourhood of £4m.

From modest beginnings the Museum has steadily expanded its computerisation resources. The number of staff employed solely in the project now stands at fifteen. A new Prime Super-mini computer not only allows for the compilation of records, but also enables curator and customer alike to answer a wide series of questions. The 600,000-odd records on the old system will be loaded into the new on-line system by the end of 1989.

In the Department of Ethnography we transferred the information on the 240,000 objects in the Department from the registers onto the computer. Then we started a process of locating the objects physically and when this has been done we shall be able to list items that are registered but not yet located, as well as items that have been located but which have lost their registration numbers. We will then marry the two sets of information. Thus we will quickly be able to provide information of all kinds about the Department's holdings, which should then provide the basis for stock-taking.

We have also been able to enter 135,000 items from the Department of Oriental Antiquities, nearly half of the 70,000 objects in the Egyptian collections, and almost a third of the estimated 600,000 in the Coins and Medals Department. The Coins and Medals program demanded a slightly different approach: the records have been compiled directly from the objects themselves and thus location codes have been added at an earlier stage. The Department of Medieval and Later Antiquities is such an extra-ordinarily diverse department that another approach has been dictated. Computer records have been created from a mixture of index cards, registers and catalogues. Nearly 30,000 objects have been entered out of an estimated total of 250,000. The four million or so items in the four departments of Greek and Roman, Western Asiatic, Prehistoric and Romano-British Antiquities and Prints and Drawings have yet to be entered.

All this takes time. The present advanced position has only been achieved by ten years of research and constant input. The British Museum is far in advance of any other museum in Europe – and perhaps in the world – if one considers both the quantity and sophistication of the methods of indexing its collections and retrieving information about them. It would be wrong to overlook this very considerable achievement by concentrating on what remains to be done. This will, of course, stretch far into the future. A crude calculation suggests that if, during the past decade, 66 man-years have been devoted to computerising 600,000 items, 600 man-years will be needed to achieve the entry of some 6,000,000 objects. With our present exiguous staff this could mean some forty years more work. Unless funding is increased we shall not, however the media and our masters huff and puff, be able to implement the ideal in a shorter period.

The difficulty of compiling a complete inventory of all the Museum's holdings for stock-taking purposes lies partly in the sheer scale of the operation. This is compounded by the problem of the expertise required to marry records with objects. No normal auditor can readily check whether, for example, one of our thousands of cuneiform tablets is that listed in the inventory: it would be difficult indeed even to find an independent cuneiform specialist in this country who would have the time to carry out such a check (the Museum employs or has employed most of the specialists in any case). How then can we do it? When questioned in 1981 by the Public Accounts Committee, even the then Comptroller and Auditor General, Sir Douglas Henley, could only say:

> honestly, in this particular sphere the normal commercial approaches to stocktaking – even in a very complex area like the Ministry of Defence with many hundreds of thousands of different pieces of equipment and so on – would not apply, for the obvious reason that although it does take a certain amount of skill, as everyone knows, to know which bit of a tank a particular piece may go into, it is not of the same order of difficulty as identification of a large number of the objects that may be in museums.

Spot checks have been made, at considerable expense of staff time, of certain items in the collection. The results have been inconclusive. The most thorough check ever made of any part of the collections was made in 1979, when during four weeks' hard work in the Department of Coins and Medals (which had to suspend all other functions for the purpose) 5 per cent of the collections was checked. Minimal losses or misplacements were discovered.

As has been frequently stressed, the most important items (with the inevitable exception of coins, medals, prints and drawings, both Western and Oriental) are on public display. The displayed objects are checked weekly (at least) by members of staff, partly to monitor their condition for conservation purposes. If they are missing they will soon be noticed. (In the twelve years since I became Director only three items have been stolen from public display: one an object on loan to a special exhibition, one an easily replaceable print on loan to the British Library and the third a minor Egyptian stone inscription which was prised from its mount by brute force on a crowded Sunday afternoon.) Objects in reserve are regularly requested by members of the general and scholarly public for examination or photography. If they are not found a thorough search is made for them. Experience has almost invariably revealed that the cause of such 'losses' is misplacement: missing items usually reappear in the wrong locations. The staff's knowledge of their own individual section of the collections forms another species of check – they would soon notice if something had gone missing. While it is not possible to quantify what percentage of the collections is checked in these ways in the course of a single year, it is certain that that proportion is high.

Realistically it is never going to be possible to audit the entire collections by stock-taking as some people imagine. The checks carried out at the moment are probably as far as we can go. As long ago as 1913 one of my predecessors, Sir Frederic Kenyon, was arguing the same case before the Public Accounts Committee. He was using arguments which are still valid today: 'the objects in the Museum', he said, 'are constantly demanded by students, and if they did not find what they wanted I should hear of it'. Perhaps the computer will help, but a computer cannot yet tell whether an Egyptian scarab with a given number is actually the one originally registered in the ledger, or whether it is a copy or a substitution.

The Museum is, however, not complacent about losses; they do occur, and are reported, and the very occasional thefts are investigated thoroughly. It is anecdotally interesting that one of the first serious investigating committees on a major theft from the coin collection in 1849 was chaired by a Trustee, Sir Robert Peel, the founder of the modern police force. In my time as

Director only one similar committee has had to be set up, when seven gold coins were stolen from the Museum by a man who was later caught. Three coins were recovered and the whole security system of the Department of Coins and Medals was thoroughly reviewed and, where necessary, tightened up. This committee was chaired by a Trustee and included senior security advisers and the most senior non-British Museum professional numismatist. Whether a computerised record will make our collections significantly more secure remains to be seen. The record will certainly, however, help the curatorial staff in their day-to-day work on the collections, and is indeed, already doing so.

At all times the security of the collections is of prime importance and the Museum's systems are significant and complex. This, however, is the one area which we cannot discuss in public – for obvious reasons. We are, however, very conscious of the dedication of our warding staff, who form our first line of defence: their loyalty is beyond question and their sense of belonging to the Museum is one of our greatest assets. An emergency procedures committee continually reviews another type of security: the threat of fire and flood, and other potential disasters. A procedural manual has been drawn up which will help in the case of a serious incident. Accidents do happen, and individual incidents which might have caused damage to the collections are carefully reviewed after the event and corrective measures put into force. We are, for the first time, shortly to run with the aid of army specialists a mock incident to test the real validity of our arrangements. Government is aware, however, that we need more money to improve our security and emergency procedures: this money must be found.

Another form of security comprises the conservation of the collections we hold. Here again a great deal of uninformed media comment has made us look like fools and even knaves. The care of the collections has both a public and a private face: in the galleries and in the storage areas. The Museum generally is not air-conditioned; this would not only be very expensive, but is also unnecessary. In certain areas – in the Clock Room (where the wooden cases of the objects are extremely delicate); in the Special Exhibitions Gallery (where loaning institutions often lay down strict conditions); in the new Japanese galleries; in the Oriental special exhibitions gallery and in the Prints and Drawings gallery – air conditioning has been, or is being, installed to protect particularly sensitive collections. In other areas, for example the room which houses the Elgin Marbles, air filtration has been introduced. The conditions needed, however, to display the varied materials from which objects are made demand local conditioning. Show-cases are, therefore, provided with different environments by means of mechanical equipment or chemical boosters. As much of our collection is displayed in such show-cases conservation considerations form an important element of exhibition planning: different conditions are required for bronzes and textiles, or wood and ivory, and so on. A special type of glass is being introduced into the roof-lights of the upper galleries, an expensive but necessary process which will reduce harmful ultra-violet and infra-red rays and solar gain, ensuring that the objects will neither fade nor dry out dangerously. Meanwhile, a protective film has been applied over existing roof-lights where it is needed.

The low light levels in our drawings exhibitions sometimes bring adverse comment, but the effect of exposure to light upon works of art on paper can be so devastating that we have to err on the side of caution. A maximum light level of 50 lux is a compromise between conservation demands to protect the objects against deterioration and the need to provide sufficient light to make them visible to the public. The levels are agreed by most authorities, both nationally and internationally: the National Trust; the Canadian Conservation Institute; the Soviet Ministry of Culture, and so on. Work on the fading of museum objects was started in the early 1950s by the United States Bureau of Standards. This has been developed, and the Bureau's recommendations modified over the years, particularly as the properties of ultra-violet light have become more clearly understood, and also as electric lamps have become more sophisticated. In some cases it has been noticed that certain changes in the materials can take place even after an item has been moved from display into dark storage (the formation of peroxy radical from a photosensitised substance in the presence of oxygen is a common example). More research is urgently needed in this field, but the standards are constantly being reviewed; indeed, the Museum is itself doing some of that research.

It should be recognised that conservation of museum objects on a scientific basis is a developing science. Even thirty years ago conservation officers had no say in exhibition planning; now they attend all the main planning meetings. They lay down lighting standards, test materials, advise on humidity levels and monitor objects on display. Curators – whilst sometimes impatient of the narrow parameters laid down by conservators – ignore conservation standards at the risk of detriment to the objects. Standards set by conservators are now being adopted world-wide and all museums must make serious efforts to adapt to these guidelines.

It is not only in the public areas that objects must be kept in conditioned environments. The Museum has a large number of storage areas built in days long before the word conservation had ever been mentioned in relation to a museum's environment. These have been upgraded over a number of years, and though there are still some difficult areas, these facilities are now in the main acceptable and are, in many instances, superior to those in other museums with large and varied collections. This is not to say that some of our cellars are not dusty or even damp, but the objects stored there will not be harmed by such conditions, although they may present to an untutored eye an appearance of neglect. Ultimately these will be dealt with, for even the appearance of neglect is often disheartening. For the moment, however, we concentrate on providing conditioned environments for such delicate materials as lacquer and leave the granite to look after itself for a little longer.

The improvement of the drains of the Museum has also had an effect on our conservation. An expensive, unglamorous programme of overhaul of the Museum's drainage system was needed to cure and stabilise conditions at and below ground level, partially to offset the effect on the fabric of the building of the rise in London's water-table since Smirke designed the foundations more than 150 years ago. This has minimised the danger of flooding and dampness in the basements.

Many of our stores are overcrowded, but this does not mean that the objects are in danger. Even the Public Accounts Committee was willing to accept that the problems of storage were containable and would be almost completely alleviated once the British Library vacated their portion of the Bloomsbury building.

Whatever care is taken of the building, of the galleries and of the storage, it is in the nature of matter that it deteriorates. It is for this reason that we have a large conservation section, one which plays a leading role in the world in trying to arrest such deterioration. The section's work is based firmly on scientific research. The collections provide the raw material for such research, which is usually problem-led. Experiment advances our knowledge of the causes and rates of deterioration of materials. This, in turn, provides the basis for the development of techniques to arrest or reverse the process of decay, even to take precautionary steps before decay sets in by recognising materials most in need of care. The ultimate aim of the conservator is to stabilise the objects with which he deals.

But we have serious problems, some of which cannot easily be resolved. Certainly the most serious is in the field of paper conservation. We are managing to contain this problem so far as Oriental paintings and prints are concerned, and are even beating back the boundaries a little. The famous Stein collection of printed paper, paintings and other materials of the first millennium AD which was recovered from caves in Chinese Central Asia has, for example, been the subject of a conservation project which is gradually revealing new treasures of Chinese art. Much more intractable is the vast problem of the Western prints. Most of our large collection of drawings is properly conserved, mounted and housed, and is subject to constant monitoring and attention. But we also have perhaps as many as two million prints, many of them unmounted, kept in folders and constantly handled by students and commercial researchers. The more valuable ones – Rembrandts, Munchs, Whistlers, Goyas, and so on – are carefully mounted and conserved, but new techniques must be developed to store in a form fit to handle the next rank of images. Many of these prints are of interest not as objects of art but as records of political or social comment, iconographical, historical or topographical detail, or simply as portraits, real or imaginary, of historical persons. This material is combed daily. If a researcher needs a cartoon to illustrate an article concerned with eighteenth-century corruption in England, a portrait of an early nineteenth-century Hungarian soldier or a view of Porlock before the invention of photography, he or she turns naturally to the British Museum. This is partly because of our policy of allowing completely free access to the collections; partly because of the expertise of the curatorial staff and the advice they provide; and partly because the Museum's collections are well sorted and convenient to handle. But in order to find an image the researchers may have to handle as many as a hundred prints and this has, over the centuries, caused many of them to become at best grubby, at worst dog-eared or torn. (It should be remembered that until recently many of the prints made in the last two centuries for popular consumption were considered of little importance and were often purchased in vast bundles for next to nothing; they were consequently often treated rather casually in the Museum.) Although students are now advised on how they should handle prints, the process of search means that they may become worn or even damaged.

It is clear that we cannot mount all two million prints, as it would be too expensive. The cost of museum-quality, acid-free mounting board alone is between £5 and £10 per image mounted, and this does not take into account the conservator's time in cleaning and repair. There are, however, other solutions. First, we can enclose prints protectively in polyester envelopes. Second, as most researchers are looking for images, it is possible to hold photographic images on microfilm, fiche and (fairly soon) on video disc. If such a programme could be set up the prints could then be kept without constant handling and issued only to those who need to examine technique or detail. This we have already practised in some areas of the collection – London topographical prints for example. But the cost in labour is prohibitively expensive in a time of financial stringency in the public area. Ultimately the money must be found for such a project, or a valuable international asset will become damaged beyond recall.

A quite separate problem concerns images on acidic paper. Until the middle of the last century all Western paper was made from rags, but with the development of a paper made from wood pulp a much cheaper method of production was introduced. Unfortunately, this paper is acidic in character and, in the wrong atmosphere, discolours or turns brittle. Careful storage can arrest the process and conservation treatment can halt it completely. But the resources needed for such conservation are almost impossible to realise. It is, therefore, necessary to invest in better storage conditions and tackle the most obvious problems in the paper conservators' laboratory. Handling is often disastrous to certain classes of paper and the temporary answer to the problem of acidic paper (until at least a less labour-intensive process of conservation is discovered) may lie in a photographic index. A more containable, but still serious, problem is provided by the fact that many prints and drawings were mounted on an acidic board, which can damage the image even if it is on handmade rag paper. This problem is tackled whenever it is recognised, but much greater resources are needed in this area as well. As for such conservation horrors as collages by Kurt Schwitters and other major twentieth-century artists, while we have to have them, we think very carefully before buying them.

The problem of paper conservation is, as mentioned above, largely one of the availability of resources. The Museum reckons that it could make considerable inroads into the problem of its own collections on paper if we were granted an extra £250,000 p.a. for staff salaries, and £150,000 p.a. for materials indexed over twenty years. This is the sort of money the government could easily provide, and the sort of money which we could certainly not raise in the private sector. We have pleaded for this money to our sponsoring department. A decision must be made.

I have already mentioned that the National Audit Office in their 1988 report criticised our inventory programme: they also discussed our conservation programme. It is fair to enlarge on some of the arguments we put before the Public Accounts Committee in order to correct an image which the press interpreted as chaos. The National Audit Office, for example, on the basis of statements provided by the Museum, noted that nine mosaics in the Museum required urgent treatment 'which it is estimated will take six man-years to carry out. A further 17 man-years work will be required to treat 22 other mosaics not in immediate danger'. What was not pointed out was that in 1981 the British Museum for the first time adapted a technique developed for other materials to the mounting of mosaics and in 1985 opened a new workshop to conserve and mount mosaics. The new technique means that the mosaics can be more easily handled and (where necessary) stored. Three of the urgent examples noted by the National Audit Office had already been treated by the time the Public Accounts Committee had considered the report and work is now in hand on the others. As a result of first aid treatment carried out since 1986 none of the mosaics is at risk.

It was this report that caused the press to pillory the Museum. We were, according to *The Times*, accused by 'the National Audit Office of scandalously neglecting the millions of works which lie unexhibited in our cellars'. The National Audit Office did no such thing, neither did the Public Accounts Committee when it reported as a result of that Office's statement. Rather, the two reports pointed to a lack of resources for the full conservation of all our collections, but recognised that we had worked hard to minimise damage and also knew exactly where the main problems of conservation lay. The National Audit Office's report recognised that we needed more storage space and we pointed out to the Public Accounts Committee that this space would become available when the British Library moved.

Sometimes the press seemed unable to read the evidence. Simon Jenkins, who appears to have little understanding of (or sympathy with) museums wrote in *The Sunday Times* under the heading 'A treasure trove rotting in the attic':

> . . . the National Audit Office delivered a devastating report suggesting that few of Britain's national museums should be entrusted with anything more than a Woolworth Tretchikoff and a set of flying ducks. At the British Museum, the inspectors found many of the 62,000 items in the cuneiform tablet collections 'beyond repair'. One hundred thousand items in the prints and drawings collection, itself 2m-3m strong, needed urgent treatment. A third of the 600 pieces languishing in the tapestry reserve were decaying.

Not a single one of these statements was true. First, we have no tapestries; second, the hundred thousand items mentioned were actually at the Victoria and Albert Museum; and what the report actually said about the cuneiform tablet collection was:

> Some 25,000 letters and fragments of the 62,000 unconserved objects in the Cuneiform Tablet Collection will need attention within the next ten years. This task will require 30 man-years of conservation work. If less urgent conservation requirements are taken into account the backlog will increase to 60 man-years. Although none of the items sampled can be categorised as being in such a bad condition that no amount of conservation can preserve them, the Conservation Department acknowledges that some such examples do exist, and that there is a risk that other tablets and fragments will enter this category.

Of course, Mr Jenkins is entitled to journalistic hyperbole, but at least he might get his facts right and perhaps he should read the reply I gave under examination by the Public Accounts Committee:

> [The NAO's point] is a totally correct statement but it should be set against the point that there are 125,000 tablets in the collection, the tablets are of unbaked clay, were used as secondary building material in the Middle East and were brought to this country many years ago. About 30 years ago we developed a method of treating these so that they could be studied, in fact it was basically baking them and removing salts from them. We were the first museum in the world to do this and have been copied by practically every other museum since. We have now done a very great number of these, well over half, and all of them have been published. The ones that have been done are all the major texts, what are left are the equivalent of King Ashurbanipal's laundry lists and are of use really only to lexicographers. In 10 to 15 years time we will have finished the conservation of these texts.

It should be repeated that our Conservation Department, hard pressed though it undoubtedly is, knows exactly what is going on in our stores; monitors them continually and takes remedial steps within the limits of our financial resources. There are few, if any, museums in the world which have the conservation resources and expertise of the British Museum and few that work harder or which have more research input. With more resources we could do much more, but the impetus must come from government.

Chapter 4
STAFF AND TRUSTEES

The British Museum curator is almost a literary paradigm – an ancient man with a long grey beard in a book-lined study, abstracted and unworldly. Nothing could be further from the truth, save that most members of the staff work in book-lined rooms. The other literary model, 'an expert at the British Museum', which is encountered in novels from Kingsley Amis to Virginia Woolf, is, however, based on experience. The Museum is a byword for art historical, antiquarian and archaeological knowledge throughout the world. It is proud of its reputation and freely gives advice on practically any artefact under the sun, even if it is only to refer the enquirer to an expert elsewhere. Dozens of letters answering enquiries are written each day; visitors' objects are identified; scholars are received and listened to; more rarified enquiries are received from official bodies or people – the Church, the police, the Foreign and Commonwealth Office, administrators of foreign museums or monuments, coroners, security advisers and so on. Some queries can be answered in two sentences: 'Your teapot was made by Wedgwood in 1780. It is a comparatively rare piece and if you wish to have it valued we would advise you to take it to one of the major auction houses'. Other queries may take hours of work and lead to academic publication either by a member of staff or by an academic colleague outside the Museum. All answers are the fruit of scholarship and experience: the British Museum expert really does exist.

The British Museum is known technically as a Non-Departmental Government Body and since the middle of the last century the Museum's staff have had the status of civil servants. This status was formalised and given emphasis in the Couzens–Hayward agreement of 1963 between the Treasury and the staff Unions, which laid down that the British Museum staff would continue to be treated in all respects as civil servants, although they are actually employees of the Trustees. Equivalence of grading with the mainstream Civil Service was achieved during the 1980s, but no recognition of the financial implications of Civil Service salary awards has been provided in the annual grant from which salaries are paid.

All curators, save the technical grades (the so-called Museum Assistants), are recruited with a university background, usually in archaeology, history or art history, but occasionally in other subjects, such as Oriental languages. Most have, by the time they have come to the Museum, published papers, finished their Ph.D or worked in another museum or in a university. They are appointed to specific posts and not to grades; it is thus unlikely that at senior level they can either move or be moved to other departments. Thus, for example, we will recruit somebody to become a specialist on Mughal art or Palaeolithic archaeology, for which subject they will have had to show some previous experience or sensitivity.

There is at the moment no shortage of good, well-trained graduates for jobs in the Museum. All must show some appreciation of material culture (the Museum wants people with an 'eye' for objects). Sometimes this means that we recruit academic staff with the most extraordinary expertises: one of our Renaissance specialists, for example, who deals chiefly with Italian maiolica, is an expert on flags. We try to recruit junior curators who have the potential to cover wide areas of material culture, who have had a serious academic post-graduate training which enables them to hold their own in the world of scholarship, and who are willing to publish at the highest academic level. At the same time we are looking for people who are prepared to take on managerial responsibility and, most importantly, are able to deal with the public. We do not always find these paragons, but we are ninety per cent successful and feel the Museum can bear it if occasionally we do find somebody who tucks himself away and writes the standard work on Polish nineteenth-century drawings.

The curators are trained on the job, mostly, it must be admitted, by osmosis. They are taught to handle objects, to use sources and records, to provide information where needed. They work closely with designers on both permanent and temporary exhibitions; they are encouraged to visit dealers and auction rooms, excavations and great houses. They usually have a number of languages and, if need be, are provided with the opportunity to learn more. They travel abroad a great deal in order to widen their knowledge (many of these trips being made on the back of other functions – accompanying loans, giving advice to foreign museums or attending conferences, all paid for by their hosts).

They are also encouraged to lecture, take visiting professorships or fellowships. They become members of the committees of learned societies, governors of British Schools of Archaeology abroad, members of university common rooms and of government committees. More senior colleagues are expected to take part in international committees and organise excavations, exhibitions or collecting trips at home and abroad. Their academic distinction – founded firmly on their day-to-day experience of the collections with which they work – is recognised by the fact that there are usually three or four members of the staff who are Fellows of the British Academy and some fifty or so who are Fellows of the Society of Antiquaries. Generally curators join the Museum for a lifetime's career, but some leave to become directors of other museums or (as I did) to become university professors. Some become dealers or join auction houses. But most people stay.

It is the excitement of working with objects, of the daily handling of them, that keeps most of us in the Museum. It is the scholarship and expertise which is built up by this deeply satisfying work that makes the Museum the great institution it is. The scholarship is expressed publicly in the Museum catalogues, in the series of texts, popular books, academic articles and guides which stream year by year from the Museum. But it is also seen in the success of our collecting and exhibition policies and in the loyalty of the staff to the institution in which they serve.

Each antiquities department is similarly structured. At the head is a person with the title of Keeper (Grade 5 in Civil Service terms). This is roughly equivalent in status and salary to a university professor, and his or her function is not unlike that of the head of a university department. Many departments – usually the bigger ones – have a Deputy Keeper who is administratively responsible for certain aspects of the department's work and acts as Keeper in the absence of the head of department. There are also a limited number of people (five at the moment) who have been promoted to Deputy Keepers on the basis of their general academic excellence (they are equivalent to university readers). The main subject areas are generally overseen by Assistant Keepers (Grade 7 in Civil Service terms), who will, for example, take charge of German drawings or Indian archaeology. One of the Assistant Keepers usually understudies the Keeper's academic interests to maintain a continuity of knowledge within the department. Staff at all levels are encouraged to go on managerial and other specialist courses of a non-academic nature.

The remaining junior academic staff are graded Curator D, E or F, and either work broadly within the departmental interests or within a narrow confine where the collections are very rich. The academic staff of the departments are supported by Museum Assistants, who are curatorial in status (which means that they are trained to handle objects) and whose main duty is to mount objects for exhibitions, move and pack them and supervise students working on the collections. The curatorial staff is backed up by executive officers, clerical officers, secretaries, messengers, technicians and, where appropriate, masons, librarians and other specialists. The Photographic Service is run centrally, with photographers seconded to individual departments (but controlled by a chief photographer) and supported by central studios and plant. (It is not without interest that the Museum employed its first photographer, Roger Fenton, in 1853, but lost him when he left for the Crimean War and became one of the most famous photographers of the mid-nineteenth century.) Curatorial departments vary in size, but the largest have as many as fifty full-time members of staff. We are not, however, prodigal either in the grading or the provision of staff. The whole Museum is subject to regular staff inspections against parameters laid down by Treasury, and the findings are implemented and staffing adjusted within our very limited resources.

The two scientific departments are staffed in a similar manner to the antiquities departments, save that their gradings are within the Civil Service scientific or conservation structure. Here we normally recruit graduates in chemistry or physics, although some have post-graduate qualifications in scientific archaeology.

The Research Laboratory undertakes the dating and scientific examination of a wide range of artefacts in collaboration with the staff of the Museum or with related outside institutions, attempting to show when, where and how objects were made and used. The Department itself initiates and takes part in excavations; the understanding of the whole history of zinc production, for example, has been changed by the work of the Department in collaboration with other institutions at Zawar in India.

The Research Laboratory is hardly paralleled in other museums and many of its services are unique. It provides routine thermoluminescence and radiocarbon dating services for many institutions. Its expertise in this latter field was recently highlighted when it served as the referee in co-ordinating the results from the various laboratories involved in the dating of the Turin Shroud. Its investigation into the sources of materials leads it into the examination of early mining and smelting sites in Spain, India, Turkey and, of course, Britain. It investigates the sources of marble used in the classical world and has consequently rewritten part of the history of our own collections. Thin-sectioning and neutron activation analysis of ceramics has established provenances of such diverse wares as Italian maiolica and Iron Age pottery found in Britain but made in central Gaul. These and many other services add to our knowledge of the material in our care. The Research Laboratory also nurses our computer and its programmes.

The twelfth department in the Museum is the Conservation Department, the work of which has been to some extent discussed in the previous chapter. It is perhaps the oldest and certainly one of the most prestigious and skilful conservation departments in the world. It is divided into five sections; paper; stone, wall-paintings and mosaics; ceramics and glass; metals and, finally, organic materials. The staff have generally studied a scientific or applied arts subject, possibly with a post-graduate diploma in conservation, and are all chosen with manual dexterity as one of their chief attributes. They are supported by a number of scientists who work on original developments – new adhesives for example – within the general field of conservation. The main tasks of the conservation officers are to monitor, repair and keep in good condition the whole of the collections and to recommend how objects should be stored and mounted. When, for example, a new exhibition is to be displayed, all the materials used within show-cases are tested to see whether they would be harmful to the objects placed on or near them. Conservation officers are often seconded to excavations run or supported by the Museum. Here they do first-aid work on the finds and more elaborate conservation work on objects being left behind in the museums of the country where the dig is taking place. The first-aid work provided in the field often saves hours of work in the laboratory or workshop on return to the Museum, especially where fragile objects have been moved by unskilled hands.

The Department has a wide reach. It takes students into its workshops from other institutions in this country and abroad, especially from Third World countries, for training in techniques and the use of materials. When major conservation problems arise outside the competence of the institution involved, the Museum is often the place from which help is sought. The Leonardo cartoon in the National Gallery (damaged by shotgun) was repaired by a British Museum conservator, as was the mace of the House of Commons when it was thrown on the floor by an irate MP; the great Derrynaflan hoard from Ireland and the St Ninian's hoard from Scotland are but two of the most delicate conservation jobs undertaken by the Department. The magnificent collection of drawings from the Cecil Higgins Museum at Bedford was mounted under contract by the Department. There is a fair turnover of staff, due to the great demand for conservation specialists in the private sector (where they may be better paid), but the hard core of loyalty met with almost everywhere in the Museum is here again evident – the attraction of the place and the variety of the jobs keep many of the staff in post.

There are in addition a number of service departments. The Design Office is brigaded with public information services – press office, education and the like – but is by far the biggest element within that department. It is headed by one of the senior designers in the country, one who holds the high distinction of being an RDI. Margaret Hall made her reputation on the memorable Tutankhamun exhibition in 1972, but had already begun to reorganise the display of our collections: her ancient glass exhibition in 1969 set new standards not only for this Museum but for

1 'The seal of the Trustees of the British Museum founded by agreement of Parliament AD 1753'. The responsibilities of the Nation to the Trustees are spelt out by this legal instrument.

2 The Museum's most important benefactor, Sir Augustus Wollaston Franks, a curator from 1851 to 1896. His catholic taste, which ranged from Celtic Britain to Japanese porcelain, backed by boundless personal generosity, led to the foundation of at least five of the Museum's present departments.

3 Holiday time at the British Museum. The Easter Bank Holiday opening of 1873 as pictured in the *Illustrated London News*. Not a particularly middle class crowd, but obviously interested in the objects.

4 Treasure galore. A glimpse of some of the 54,951 third-century coins found in the Roman town of Cunetio (Wiltshire). Processed and cleaned by the Museum, and declared Treasure Trove, the hoard was published within five years of its discovery.

5 The British Museum conducts a number of excavations abroad: Tell es-Sa'idiyeh in Jordan is one of the most important. Here may be seen the main excavation area on the upper mound, looking west towards the River Jordan in 1989. The corner of the twelfth-century BC Egyptian Governor's Residency, excavated in 1987, appears in the foreground, behind which work starts on the isolation of the ninth-century BC city level.

6 (*Right*) The National Heritage Memorial Fund is now the greatest single benefactor of the Museum. In 1989, for example, it gave £200,000 towards the purchase price of £377,000 for the Cosway Salt, a piece of English plate hallmarked London 1584-5. Once the property of the artist Richard Cosway, it is one of the rarest and most ambitious types of Elizabethan salt and is in superlative condition. The National Art-Collections Fund and the Pilgrim Trust also contributed to the purchase.

7 Drawing by Guido Reni, *Christ on the Cross*, a finished study for the altarpiece painted 1617-18 for the Capuchin church outside Bologna. Bought in 1987 for £2,500 and only attributed to Guido Reni, scholarship enabled the Museum to buy this most traditional of museum items at a knock-down price from an established London dealer.

8 Japan in Bloomsbury. A corner of the Oriental paper conservation workshop.

9 Late nineteenth-century taste produced crowded galleries and overflowing cases. Here a 'Victorian style' ethnographic gallery provides mind-blowing possibilities of confusion between continents.

10 and 11 Smirke's original cases still in situ in the gallery devoted to the Greeks in Southern Italy (*top*). The glazing bars inhibit the exhibition, and their refurbishment was as expensive as the installation of brand new show-cases. Next door (*bottom*) the A. G. Leventis Gallery of Ancient Cyprus demonstrates modern cases (capable of being air-conditioned internally) and modern display techniques which will last for at least twenty years. Heating was introduced from the ceiling into a gallery which had had no central heating since 1930.

12 Bomb damage at the head of the central staircase, May 1941. Although the area has now been reconstructed as galleries, the skylights were not replaced and the roofs were merely covered with roofing felt. Within the next ten years these roofs will need to be rebuilt.

13 The queues for Tutankhamun, the first 'blockbuster' exhibition never to be repeated.

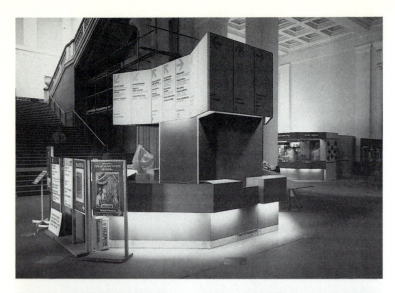

14 and 15 The Front Hall has been the target of designers for years. In the
early 1970s it was dominated by an enormous information point which
filled too much floor space and was less than efficient (*top*). The cleared
central area (*bottom*) now allows freer movement, and the information
panel at the back of the hall draws visitors into the building, thus
avoiding crowding just inside the front door.

16 'The Living Arctic' was a major exhibition of the Department of Ethnography. Interactive video discs provided by Indigenous Survival International were used with great effect as a touch-screen information point. Splendid in a temporary exhibition, but distracting and difficult to service in a permanent gallery. (Photo: New Media Productions Ltd)

17 This picture is not posed! Students of cuneiform and other cognate material working in the Students' Room of the Department of Western Asiatic Antiquities in the summer of 1987. The servicing of such students forms a major part of the curatorial duties of each department.

18 An important Research Laboratory project examines metal production sites all over the world. Here one of a bank of seven medieval furnaces for zinc extraction excavated at Zawar Mala, India. The retorts in which the zinc is distilled rest on a perforated clay plate.

19 The process of fund-raising. David Wilson, Lawrence Smith and Teruko Iwanaga in the offices of *Asahi Shimbun* in Tokyo on one of many short fund-raising visits to Japan.
(Photo: *Asahi Shimbun*)

20 (*Right*) Fund-raising blessed. A Shinto priest (perhaps the first one ever to perform a Shinto religious ceremony in Britain) blesses the site of the new Japanese galleries in a traditional ground-breaking ceremony.

21 The reconstructed façade of the late nineteenth-century palace of the Asante kings at Kumasi, Ghana, formed the centre piece of the Asante exhibition at the Museum of Mankind.

22 A corner of the public restaurant. The food is surprisingly good.

the country as a whole. The designers work in teams who deal with three-dimensional, graphic and editorial questions (alongside curators and conservators) to provide both temporary and permanent exhibitions. Here again there is a significant turnover of staff, but the senior members tend to resist the temptation of greener grass outside. (Their work and philosophy is discussed further in chapter 5.)

The education office is small but important. Its main job is to provide teaching materials for schools, and there is an enormous demand for its services. Some two thousand school parties are annually serviced by the provision of education packs and other facilities and untold numbers of informal visits are also made by schoolchildren from this country and abroad. One of the members of the section has taken a special interest in disabled problems and, indeed, served as administrator to the Attenborough Committee which published in 1985 and 1988 two reports on the arts and the disabled. In the Museum much has been done to improve access and other provision for disabled visitors, including two 'touch' exhibitions designed for the partially sighted and blind.

The section also runs a major public lecture programme which reaches an audience of some twenty thousand people each year: nearly ten thousand people attend individual gallery talks and fourteen thousand our film and video shows. It puts on courses in association with the Open University, art schools, teacher training institutes and polytechnics; it runs a loan exhibition service for schools, universities and museums; it organises film shows and such practical and demonstration classes as may be provided in the Department of Ethnography by craftsmen from other countries invited to London for the purpose. Gallery lectures are supplemented by official guided tours and the Education Office works closely with the Trustees' publishing company, British Museum Publications, in initiating specialist educational literature.

The general administrative side of the Museum has been honed to a fine edge over the years. Presided over by a senior officer (Grade 5) recruited from the Treasury (on the principle that poachers need a gamekeeper on their side), he controls sections covering finance, contracts, accounts, personnel, office services and management services (including internal audit and staff inspection). He is also responsible for the Works and Security Departments and the Photographic Service.

Since 1988 the Museum has taken over responsibility for the upkeep of its various buildings from the Property Services Agency and a Department of Architectural and Building Services has been constructed to deal with this added dimension to our activities. Headed by an architect, its professional staff are now able to undertake the supervision of all the building works (including maintenance) on the site without working through the intermediary of the old Agency. This has led to much greater flexibility, which, as we gain in experience, will increase our efficiency immeasurably.

The administrative division of the Museum has been carefully built up over twenty years (after a management survey by outside specialists) to become an efficient and workmanlike institution which acts as a model to many other museums. Our staff inspectors and internal auditors are much sought after and work on contract for other institutions. (The head of our staff inspection unit – originally a member of the staff of the education service – was not only trained by the Treasury Management Unit but was also the chief consultant with them in drawing up official grading guidance for national museum staff throughout the country.) The Museum has been scrutinised in various areas of its management processes over the last few years at the behest of the Office of Arts and Libraries and has not yet been accused of either inefficiency or overmanning. The administration has to be efficient, as it provides services for a staff which approaches 10 per cent of the total workforce of museums – national and provincial – in Great Britain.

A small administrative department, the Secretariat, deals with legal matters, services Trustee committees, controls the central archives and registry and runs the central library (most of the books in the Museum are, however, controlled by the departments).

The whole Museum is run by the Director and Deputy Director, who form the public face of the Museum. The Director is the accounting officer for the Museum and is, therefore, ultimately responsible for all the Museum's functions. Both the Director and Deputy Director are academics, and the academic leadership given by the directorate is seen by the Trustees as one of its most important functions. This leadership is important in that the Director must be able to grasp the problems raised by the curatorial departments on a day-to-day basis. He or she must be able to judge matters of acquisition, publication, fieldwork and international co-operation, make judgments on display and publicity which often take the Museum into controversial areas, and also, cautiously, be a public figure, dealing with the media and the international community.

The Director also has a considerable representational role, particularly of recent years, in relation to fund-raising, which has become an increasingly important part of the job. As a leading member of the international museum community, the Director's activities are often carried out abroad, and the balance between these functions and the general administration of the Museum is one of extremely fine judgement in which the support of the Deputy Director and the general administration of the Museum are of paramount importance.

The main management group of the Museum, therefore, consists of the Director, Deputy Director and the head of administration. There are a few formal internal committees which meet regularly, particularly in such complicated fields as Buildings and Design. There is also a regular meeting of senior management with the heads of the antiquities and scientific departments. Otherwise, the management group meets as and when necessary with the relevant officers to deal with more complicated matters raised by the various sections of the administration. The main Trades Unions within the Museum are those of the Civil Service, relations with which are formalised through the Whitley Council structure.

The individual antiquities departments are semi-autonomous (their Keepers in moments of impatience have been branded as satraps!). On the whole their business is easily devolved from the centre. Each department has its own annual budget, and only three areas are administered centrally: staff and salaries; buildings and maintenance; and major purchases (the first of these we are considering devolving within the next few years). Each department has a students' room. Here the scholar is received and assisted, and supervised in his or her handling of material. The students' rooms of the departments of Coins and Medals and Prints and Drawings have been elaborately planned to meet the security and conservation demands of the material; in other cases the room is rather more like an open-plan office, with junior staff supervising from their permanent desks. In this way we have rather well-developed systems; many departments in other large museums have no such facilities. In the Metropolitan Museum in New York, for example, a student may well have to squash into the tiny office of a curator in order to study a medieval reliquary, while in some departments of the Victoria and Albert Museum the student has to work at the desk of an absent member of staff.

The level of service provided in these rooms depends entirely on the level of demand. Quite frequently the requests simply encompass bringing specified items to the student's table. In other cases a curator may spend hours discussing knotty problems of attribution with an international scholar. Another aspect of the services provided for the public deals with requests for the identification of objects. This often entails the production of photographs or literature, even occasionally furnishing comparative material to point an argument, but curators never ultimately begrudge time spent in this process because they accumulate experience through it. They quite frequently catch sight of – and sometimes even acquire – new, unique or specialist items which illuminate their own subject. By answering a casual public enquiry of this sort, for example, the Museum was able to buy (after the vendor had had an independent valuation) a gem-like Carolingian ivory – an extremely rare object, of the importance of which the owner knew nothing. Dealers often acknowledge advice by making special prices or letting the Museum have first refusal on items bought for stock. Even if the Museum does not want to acquire an item, handling, for example, an indifferent icon will certainly increase the curator's knowledge of his own subject and a photograph may be added to our archive as a consequence which will be of use to future generations of curators and to outside scholars working in the field.

Enquiries received by letter from both scholar and amateur take up a good deal of time, but fulfil the same function. The Department of Ethnography has absorbed the library of the Royal Anthropological Institute and this consequently, by the agreement reached between the Institute and the Museum, serves as a national specialist library in this field; its physical situation also familiarises visiting scholars with the work of the departmental curators and vice versa.

Our collections are completely open to scholar and amateur alike and, although we could never make the collections completely open for handling, only the most frivolous enquirer will be politely sent away. We deal sympathetically also with the naive. There was, for example, a Christmas Eve on which I was the only curatorial member of the Department on duty when two Canadians came and asked to see the wedding-ring of Joseph and Mary, which they were convinced was in the British Museum. They were devout fundamentalists, they could not be treated with contempt; half an hour with them taught lessons in tact and humility. Such an experience in one shape or form is shared by every curatorial member of the staff of the Museum and many of its warders and information staff.

The curators must also make the collections available for display. Most however, are hopeless at this and should never be let loose on their own, otherwise the labels would be too specialised and the cases too crowded and undisciplined. They must provide the brief and the material for the designers and work with them as amicably as possible. The curators also initiate special exhibitions, either of the Museum's own material or by loan from other museums.

The third way in which the curator makes the collection available is through publication. The great museum catalogue series referred to in the first chapter are still produced and form a unique platform of scholarship in material culture referred to by specialists throughout the world. Between eight and twelve of these are produced each year by both curators and outside scholars. Recent titles published by the Trustees' publishing company include: *Catalogue of Demotic Papyri* vol. III; *Catalogue of the Excavated Prehistoric and Romano-British Material in the Greenwell Collections; Sylloge of Coins of the British Isles – Athelstan to the Reform of Edgar 924–973* and *Catalogue of Greek and Roman Glass* vol. I. More informal and immediate scholarly publications are the Occasional Papers produced in-house and sold on a non-commercial basis. These books range from the 'proceedings' of symposia to preliminary excavation reports and monographs of very specialist interest, such as *A Study of Ancient Egyptian Cordage in the British Museum.*

Less specialist, but also deeply scholarly are the frequent catalogues or books produced for exhibitions which increasingly form the basis of new scholarship in particular fields and also provide the non-specialist with an introduction to an unknown subject. Among recent titles are *Archaeology in Britain since 1945; The Shadow of the Guillotine, Britain and the French Revolution; Florentine Drawings of the Sixteenth Century*, and *Süleyman the Magnificent*. More general publications encompass all-purpose guides, small popular books on subjects as diverse as Celtic art, clocks and watches, and runic writing; general monographs on such subjects as ethnic jewellery, Buddhism, ancient Egypt and Roman Italy. Through these books the name and expertise of the Museum is carried into bookshops all over the world. British Museum Publications also produce children's books and guides for visitors of all ages.

The official publication programme of the Museum is closely monitored and encouraged by the Scholarship Committee of the Board of Trustees. All academic work is scrutinised by the Committee, scholarly publications are approved, and seminars and symposia reported on. This Committee also looks at information retrieval for scholarly purposes through computers and word processors, receiving reports from the internal staff committee working on information technology. There is a clear future for the use of the computer in place of some of the published catalogues, but the technology which will allow this, and the will to use it, are still some way away, and books seem destined to remain for some time an inevitable element of the Museum scholar's apparatus.

The twenty-five Trustees of the Museum whose composition is described above (p. 14), comprise the great and the good: a royal duke, a few peers, a sculptress, a handful of senior academics, an industrialist, businessmen, retired public servants, a senior architect, a QC and so on (four of them are women). They meet on Saturdays, a great convenience to all busy men, save for the Chairman of the Horse Race Betting Levy Board who sometimes has calls on his time elsewhere. Meetings are held at five or six weekly intervals, save during August and September. The Trustees elect their own Chairman (presently Lord Windlesham) from amongst their own membership, which gives continuity to their decisions, to the policies of the Board and to the Museum's sense of direction.

The Trustees decide matters of policy on the recommendation of the Director and senior staff. The meetings are structured so that generally the only non-strategic decisions taken concern the acquisition of objects. At each meeting a head of department delivers an annual report of work done, and is questioned about the departmental work. In turn the Keeper puts his or her views on the general direction of Trustees' policy as it affects the department. (Trustees have had the opportunity to visit the department before the meeting at which the report is presented.) The Board works by consensus; in nearly thirteen years as Director I have only known one vote to be taken. It is enormously impressive in the way in which it deals with business; the administration attempts to place incisive documents before the Board and discussion of them is mostly at a very high level with the background of much experience. Trustees are normally appointed for terms of five years. This is renewable, but no Trustee is appointed or renewed after the age of seventy (in practice about sixty-eight). Trustees are good attenders – there are rarely more than three or four absentees – and they happily meet senior staff after each meeting informally over a buffet lunch. Before each Board Meeting there is a display of recent or proposed acquisitions and opportunity is given for individual Trustees to consult the curatorial staff informally concerning the objects displayed.

There are a number of sub-committees of the Board. The Scholarship Committee's work has already been mentioned: other committees deal with Finance (with an investment sub-committee to monitor the Museum's small private trust funds); Public Services (which monitors fund-raising, education, publicity, the restaurants and the general public face of the Museum); Buildings and Design (perhaps the committee which is more executive than any other), Excavation and Fieldwork Committee, a Committee on Scientific Research and Conservation, and a Staff Committee, which meets only to consider matters of policy concerning conditions of employment (general staff matters are left strictly to management). Each Committee meets generally twice a year, more rarely quarterly.

The Trustees recommend the name of a new Director to the Prime Minister. They approve the appointment of a new head of department on the basis of the recommendation of an interview board run by the Civil Service Commission which includes at least one Trustee. The hard and regular work put in by Trustees is a measure both of the support they give the Museum and also of their affection for the Museum itself. Almost every Trustee who retires from the Board feels that it is one of the most satisfying institutions he or she has worked for: they depart with great reluctance. The staff of the Museum respect the Trustees, not only because they are considerable public personages, but because they take a real interest in the work of the Museum and are seen to support the Museum in public and private. To the Director, as to the staff, the Trustees are seen as a protection against outside interference in the running of the Museum, either by Whitehall or by ill-informed public opinion expressed through the press or media. The Trustees in a real sense hold the Museum and its collections in trust for the international community, as they have done since 1753.

The Trustees own the commercial arm of the Museum, having capitalised it out of their private funds. Known as British Museum Publications, the company was originally founded to ginger up the production of the learned catalogues of the Museum, which had fallen into the doldrums, mainly because of the comparative inertia of the official government publication process which had then to be used.

The function of producing the learned publications of the Museum remains the first charge on the Company, and over the years the Company has saved the Nation hundreds of thousands of pounds in this area. The Company also runs the Museum's shops, which sell souvenirs and books. The bookshop is a major outlet for literature about art and archaeology, selling a wide range of other publishers' books as well as the Museum's own publications. The souvenir end of the commercial concern is highly successful and we are flattered (as well as annoyed) to find that some of our products are copied in rather inferior form by competitors in other countries. The Company has a turnover of nearly £4m per year and (after the learned catalogues have been paid for) profits go to the Trustees. When the departure of the British Library makes more space available, we look forward to expanding our retail areas and doubling the turnover. Nowadays commercial operations are normal adjuncts of Non-Departmental Public Bodies, but it is interesting to note that as late as 1975 the Public Accounts Committee examined this at that time very unusual operation to see that no public subsidy went into what was in effect a private company. They found that the Museum was playing by the rules, particularly as the Company pays rent to the Museum for that part of the premises it occupies and thus substantially contributes to the public purse.

Other associated concerns run or supported by the Museum include the British Museum Development Trust, a financial vehicle for fund-raising, and the British Museum Society, which acts as a supporters' club and helps us with financial and moral support. The Society has six thousand members, who enjoy certain privileges such as free admission to paying exhibitions, a members' room, organised lectures, tours and openings. It also publishes a periodical which aims at a wider public. It is a source for volunteer help when the Museum needs it: members act as stewards in exhibitions for the blind or as interviewers during museum surveys, for example. We are also tentatively trying a new commercial venture, specialist tours abroad of an archaeological or cultural nature.

In the course of this chapter I have attempted to explain the complicated staffing and administrative structure of a great national institution. The picture has been painted with a very broad brush: it has been impossible to mention those who do a multitude of minor jobs which all help to make the Museum run relatively smoothly: the man who scrapes discarded chewing-gum from the floor; the man who looks after the Museum's cats (necessary animals for discouraging vermin and pigeons); the man who mends wheelbarrows; the first-aid specialists who cope with minor accidents and illnesses; the Welfare Department, which looks after the staff's problems, or the resident engineer who knows how every drain, pipe, wire, switch or electrical plant can be controlled in an emergency. The Museum works seven days a week, twenty-four hours a day to provide a service to the public and to scholarship alike.

Chapter 5

THE BUILDINGS AND THE PUBLIC

The Museum was built by government and private benefactors for the benefit of the public, to store and display the collections. Such a sentence states the obvious, but in days of a rampant preservation lobby its purpose is often forgotten and the complications of running a Grade I listed building which plays host to four million visitors each year have been consistently ignored by those who could have helped us in the past. It is sad and typical that the Museum still suffers from war damage, hastily repaired by successive cheese-paring administrations. Only in the last few years has there been any attempt to face up to the problem and there is still a long way to go. The main Bloomsbury building is arguably the greatest Greek Revival building in the country, it is itself a worthy object of pilgrimage. Consequently it needs careful attention and a considerable amount of money spent on it. It is a vast complex; it stands on almost 5 hectares of ground, it has over 3 hectares of roofs and 4 kilometres of public gallery space.

The galleries should – and in most cases do – form a fitting back-drop against which to display some of the world's greatest treasures in a manner both intelligible to the visitor and respectful of the building. Fortunately, the architect who designed the building designed it as a museum; it is not – like the Louvre in Paris or the State Hermitage Museum in Leningrad – a sanitized palace. It was seen as a temple to natural history and to artefacts made by man, built in a long tradition of such buildings, both in this country and abroad. The classical temple was a model for such earlier buildings as the original Hunterian Museum in Glasgow (1804) and Barry's City Art Gallery in Manchester (1823), and it continued to be the model for many of the later nineteenth-century public galleries and museums (the Royal Scottish

Academy, the Fitzwilliam Museum at Cambridge and the Ashmolean Museum at Oxford are but a few of them). The same idea can be seen abroad; the Altes Museum in Berlin and the Glyptothek in Munich also formed temples in the same tradition, as (much later) did the National Gallery in Washington. The carved tympanum of the British Museum, by Sir Richard Westmacott stressed this idea, representing Man emerging from a rude savage state, through the influence of religion. The emergence of the arts, drama, poetry and music and science are balanced by the natural world in an iconography which defies and has defied description since it was erected.

The main building, designed and executed under the supervision of Sir Robert Smirke, has been much added to since it was finished in 1849. First, there was the magnificent round Reading Room designed by Sydney Smirke and completed in 1857, which destroyed the whole interior logic of the original building; then the White Wing was added on the site of the Principal Librarian's garden on Montague Street, the Assyrian galleries and Mausoleum Room being added to the west range. These were designed by Sir John Taylor in what Professor Mordaunt Crook, the historian of the Museum's buildings, has described as the 'chastest Greek Revival'. After the move of the natural history departments to South Kensington in the 1880s the Museum drew breath and no further building was completed until the King Edward VII building, designed by Sir John James Burnet, was opened in 1914. This was intended to be the first stage in a major addition which would have surrounded the whole of Smirke's building and solved our accommodation problems for a long time to come. The King Edward VII Building is very much underestimated as architecture: it is described by Sir John Summerson as 'directly in the tradition of Duc's Palais de Justice and Ginain's library at the Ecole de Medicine. His colonnade is brilliantly handled – stretched like a screen from one massive pylon to another, overlapping the pylons at each end in such a way as to give the colonnade all the dignity of independence while relating it harmoniously to a building of fundamentally modern character'. Hidden in the roof space of this building are the series of Japanese galleries which have been created out of nothing and will be opened in 1990.

The next major construction project after the King Edward VII

Building was the Duveen Gallery. Funded through the generosity of Lord Duveen for rehousing the Parthenon sculptures, this building was designed by the American architect John Russell Pope (who was responsible for the National Gallery of Art in Washington). Although completed in 1939 the gallery was not then occupied and its stone cladding was shattered by a bomb in 1940. It finally opened to the public in 1962. The only other substantial addition since then has been a functional wing for offices, special exhibition gallery, restaurant and Board-Room, designed by Professor Colin St John Wilson and built at public expense in the 1970s. Planning permission and financial stringencies curtailed the original plan for this extension, so that the public areas are far too small for the purposes for which they were originally intended.

Over the years individual needs, emergencies and changing taste have allowed untidiness and excrescences to negate the original architectural purity. In the 1870s, for example, the Front Hall was extended with great loss of architectural dignity and, more important, of daylight, whilst in the mid-1960s the latest of a series of hideous accretions was created to hold the Bassae Frieze by inserting a half-mezzanine into an important Smirke gallery (one which originally held the Parthenon sculptures).

It is important to understand the building history of the Museum, as it explains many of the problems we encounter today. The Museum is essentially a Regency building; a building of light and shade, in the main cool and austere and intended to be full of daylight. The roof-lights of the upper galleries and the long windows of the Egyptian Sculpture Gallery form a major architectural component of the Museum's design. Artificial light was not introduced into the Museum, for fear of fire, until 1879, when the Museum purchased its first electrical generator to light the Reading Room. The Museum was built with central heating, and the floors, particularly downstairs, were designed to take the great weights of sculpture at that time appearing from the classical world, Egypt and the Middle East. Members of Smirke's office had designed a series of wall-cases (some of these can be seen in Room 73), but glass technology was not sufficiently advanced for them to have been manufactured without glazing bars. Smirke's design was gradually modified, the last development being seen in the Chinese and Indian galleries of the King Edward VII

Building (1914), which are perhaps the most easily adaptable to modern display purposes.

Although purpose built, the Museum still has many problems. At the time of the opening of the main building it was condemned by the critics as being unadventurous and out-of-date. But, as it had taken thirty years to build in a period when high Victorian taste was developing, this is hardly surprising. The 'rational, austere and economical' design of the Museum was deemed tame and lacking in ornament; it was taken to task for its, 'formalised deformity, shrivelled precision and starved accuracy', and described as a 'miserable abortion'. So it was immediately embellished to make it more interesting, according to the taste of the time, by an extraordinary decorative programme which denied all Robert Smirke's original ideas and which has come back to haunt us today. The building of the Reading Room caused considerable and continuous inconvenience to the general public in that visitors still cannot pass on the ground floor from the north to the south side. Even the floor levels of the King Edward VII Building are not in register with the Smirke building on any floor. It is thus a complicated museum round which to direct the public. The Front Hall, enlarged twenty years after the Reading Room had been constructed, is far too small: at certain times of the year it cannot accommodate the vast numbers pouring into it. However hard we try, we cannot persuade visitors to use the North Entrance. To compound this difficulty we have in many galleries built-in wall-cases totally unsuitable for modern display purposes. The alteration of these or indeed of any public part of the building demands approaches to the planning authorities. We alter the building at our peril from the amenity societies. But as an institution pledged to preserve the past, we must continually defend the fabric from cultural prejudice.

On a different plane of difficulty is the problem of access. The British Museum is not easy to find; it is basically a back-street museum, although it was never intended to be so. Indeed, it was always intended to be the focal point of a grand vista either from Trafalgar Square or from Waterloo Bridge. Various schemes were put forward for the fulfilment of this ideal, the latest being the scheme of Sir Leslie Martin and Professor Wilson, which was ignominiously abandoned by government in 1967. The Martin–Wilson scheme caused planning blight, not only in that area of

Bloomsbury which was to have been pulled down, but also in the Museum building itself, as repairs were not undertaken, decisions were delayed and the Museum neglected. The only 'gain' from the government's rejection of this plan was provision for out-housing the Department of Ethnography in the Museum of Mankind. This was placed in an edifice built between 1866 and 1869 as the pompous Senate House of the University of London in Burlington Gardens; it has a worthy exterior, but is highly unsuitable as a museum building. The difficulties caused by the physical nature of this building are compounded by the fact that it is also difficult to find and that it separates an essential element of the Museum from its main collections.

Successive governments and their agencies have refused to face up to the problems of the Bloomsbury building – with apparent justification since the costs are high. Even at their most grandiloquent moments, as for example at the time when the King Edward vii Building was built, corners were cut. The ventilation shafts in this building were lined with inferior materials and the sub-basement was inadequately drained, despite pleas on the part of the architects. By far the worst neglect was, as we have seen, in the period after the Second World War, when bomb-damage was left unrepaired for decades: temporary roofs still cover some of the once burnt-out galleries and, what is more, deny them the daylight so important to Smirke's architecture. As late as the 1950s and 1960s duckboards crossed rooms 69 and 70, which were still open to the sky, and only in 1990 will we actually restore the Smirke ceiling of the latter (the ceiling and roof of the former is a problem for my successor!).

When the New Wing was completed in 1979 the Trustees and the Directorate made a compact with our sponsor department that we would attempt no more new building unless it was privately funded and would turn our attention to maintenance – repairing and bringing up to standard the whole structure. This was an unexciting programme and indeed it was done in the teeth of official forward planning figures (pesc) unfavourable to all the national museums in London. This daunting task is still incomplete, but we are gradually making inroads into the problem.

A few examples will suffice to illustrate the story. Even in the late 1970s it was common to see scattered around the galleries in time of rain small piles of sawdust or even buckets under leaks in the skylights. It had always been so and none thought it strange. These monuments to inadequate maintenance have now disappeared as the glazing has been repaired. What is not, however, so evident is that in many cases whole roof lanterns have been replaced and special glass which filters harmful ultra-violet and infra-red light is being introduced. The main drainage system, which caused storm-water floods and worse, has been inspected, renewed where necessary and maintained on a regular basis for the first time since the Second World War. A new electrical ring-main and sub-stations are presently being installed at a cost in excess of £1.5m. A new telephone system was installed and financed by holding posts vacant. The façades of the building have been cleared of their London grime, not simply to restore their former purity but also so that damaged stone could be replaced. As a result of this work it was discovered that the west pediment of the east wing had shifted and was dangerous; this had to be rebuilt.

The completion of the cleaning of the front of the Museum, however, was a tonic to all who worked in it: they felt less shabby, less neglected. The magnificent railings cast by John Walker and Co. of York in 1852 were showing signs of serious deterioration: they were stripped down to the raw metal, repaired and repainted in Brunswick green (their traditional, though not their original, colour). The spikes were repaired and regilded at a cost of £10,000 (the original gilding cost £385). Car-parking was banned beneath the portico, and the area in front of the steps laid out with much-needed seating for visitors. A new south-west gateway was designed and installed. The Museum had not looked so grand, clean or imposing since it was built.

The external cleaning was balanced inside. A rolling programme of gallery redecoration was introduced and untidy corners were cleaned out; clutter and rubbish was removed from basement corridors and a programme of reorganising storage put in hand. All this was done quietly with support from the Office of Arts and Libraries, but as building costs escalated in London so the programme has slowed down and we still face serious problems of underfunding for maintenance: the whole building needs to be completely rewired; certain aspects of the security system need to be renewed; the north forecourt allows water through to a major basement and needs urgent attention; the surface of the front forecourt is breaking up and in any case needs to be replaced by something more in keeping with the great building it introduces; the bomb-damaged roofs, which were inadequately replaced, need to be rebuilt at vast expense; the lecture theatre ventilation system is worn out and needs replacement; staff accommodation is seriously in need of improvement; 150 metres of upper galleries need floor strengthening, and so on. Not all this can be done at once, but some £20m will be needed before 1996 in order to bring the building up to normal good-housekeeping standards, and it will be extremely difficult to raise the extra money needed for the floor strengthening.

In 1988, as we have seen, the Museum untied itself from the Property Services Agency (the official building and works arm of government), and, although a few of the longer-running contracts are still administered by the Agency, the Museum can now control its own works in a more direct and efficient manner. The new system will not cost any less but, with luck, more can be done and it can be done more quickly. We now have our own architects and clerks of works who can deal with contractors and tackle problems as they arise without cutting their way through miles of red tape. In our first year we seem to have made few blunders, and although our architects' staff has worked amazingly long hours all have gained inspiration from the vistas of new responsibilities opened up for them.

We have long had a design department which wrested responsibility for the interior design from the PSA in the late 1970s. This is the department which most influences the visitor to the Museum, as it produces the displays both temporary and permanent, which are what the public comes to see. The Department's job is to avoid over-design and overcrowding; to display the collections with minimum interference to enjoyment and appreciation; to provide, as discreetly as possible, information about an object itself and the context in which it belongs, and to offer a quiet, unobtrusive ambience in which the public are not disturbed by externals. Not an easy task within an important historic building. The Design Office also advises on colour schemes for the public areas, on general lighting, on furnishing, carpeting, flooring and show-case design. They have devised a house style for labelling, and have avoided the temptation of all public relations consultants and even some designers to produce a logo for the Museum!

The last gallery not designed by the Design Office was the refurbished Egyptian Sculpture Gallery (room 25), which was opened by the Prime Minister in 1981. But already by that time house-style labelling had been developed by our own designers and was used here for the first time in a new permanent display. Since that date more than forty galleries have been relabelled, either because they had been remodelled or because the information given was insufficient and out of date. Before 1992 a dozen or so galleries will have been redesigned or rebuilt with house-style labelling, and the rest of the Museum's galleries will have been relabelled by the time the Library leaves the building in 1996. Labelling is an expensive process, in terms of both cash and designers' time, but the results are well worthwhile.

There are three levels of labelling: gallery identification, information panels which set the objects in context, and labels for individual items. The labels or information panels must not dominate either the gallery or the displayed objects. We try not to write a book on the wall or in the show-cases, as few people have the concentration to read long wall-panels. Objects are, however, set in context, sometimes with a picture, sometimes with a map or drawing. On in-case labels in permanent galleries (one is illustrated in fig. 2) there is normally a rather bold introductory sentence, followed by any necessary explanation in a slightly less emphatic type-face and form. Technical detail (donor, registration number and so on) is printed in a small type-face; such information is needed by scholars and the former meets obligations to donors. Labels cannot always be placed so as to relieve viewers of the need to move their heads, but such a necessity is rarely onerous. The type-face and its size have been carefully chosen to be read by all who wear spectacles; labels are usually set at levels which require no bending on the part of the visitor, but this cannot always be achieved, particularly when labels are mounted on bases on which pieces of sculpture stand. It should be said, however, that many of the complaints made about illegible labelling come from middle-aged people like myself whose reading glasses have not been renewed for years! We are proud of our labelling and any visitor who has recently tried to identify pictures on the upper line in the Grand Gallery of the

Limestone portrait head from a statue of a woman
Made in Cyprus, around 300 BC
From the sanctuary of Apollo at Pyla

Her features resemble those of Berenice I (about 340 to before 275 BC), wife of Ptolemy I, king of Egypt and ruler of Cyprus.

Given by A W Franks
GR 1871.5-6.1 (Sculpture C 366)

Fig. 2. A standard label (actual size).

Louvre by means of their labels will remember that we have come a long way from the similar small uninformative typewritten labels in the British Museum of thirty years ago.

Model reconstructions are rarely used to explain the use of an object, save in special exhibitions; most objects can easily be explained by graphics on information panels. I fight a constant battle with some curators on this point, but generally there is agreement that the public wants to see the original object, is intelligent enough to understand a drawing and does not need a model – which in any case takes up much-needed space. It was interesting that on the one occasion on which push-button, electronically illuminated maps were introduced into a permanent exhibition they were largely ignored and no one complained at their removal. Interactive videos are, however, a great success in special exhibitions, as are other types of audio-visual displays, particularly computer graphics, but they cannot easily be introduced into permanent exhibitions as maintenance is difficult and expensive.

Provision for exhibitions of the type of object collected by the British Museum is not cheap. If it is a heavy piece of sculpture, then it has to be moved, and we have an experienced team of masons who are used to moving anything large and unwieldy. When, for example, the Egyptian Sculpture Gallery was redesigned in the late 1970s every single piece of sculpture, including the colossal head of Rameses II weighing some 7.4 tonnes, was moved and some were reset on new bases. But for the moment we have finished reorganising the sculpture galleries and are concentrating instead on the first-floor galleries where, partly for load-bearing reasons, most of the material displayed is more portable. Consequently, it has to be locked up, and not only locked up, but placed in conditioned environments, which can only be provided within sophisticated modern cases. Such showcases are expensive: a free-standing showcase able to endure the wear and tear encountered in the Museum and capable of being adapted for a mini-environment costs about £3,000 per metre. Thus the refurbishment of a gallery 200 square metres long will cost, with the minimum works element some £250,000. A large gallery like the one which will house the permanent exhibition 'Rome, City and Empire' (for which we have a most generous grant from the Wolfson Foundation), will cost over one million pounds, as the temporary roof has to be replaced.

After a number of years of experiment the Museum has now got into its stride, and the designs of the A. G. Leventis Gallery of Cypriot Antiquities and the John Addis Islamic Gallery are a foretaste of what visitors will see in all the so-far unreformed upper galleries, particularly those belonging to the Egyptian and Western Asiatic Departments. The Trustees hope to refurbish all these before the Museum takes over the vacated British Library space in 1996.

Permanent exhibitions, like temporary exhibitions, are co-operative efforts. The brief is prepared by the scholar responsible for the collection to be displayed and handed to the designer, who then works to cut down the impossible number of items that all curators wish to show in an exiguous space. The Conservation

Department has to be satisfied that conditions are correct for display, and heating systems have often to be repaired so that warders and public do not freeze in the winter. As Director I chair meetings which resolve disputes in all these conflicting areas, but generally the work is done amicably, with good relations between all parties.

Fashions change in exhibition techniques and presentation, as in everything else. At the present the Museum is trying to adopt a classic style which is comparatively ageless. We intend to return the Museum's galleries to the rooms envisaged by Smirke, removing false ceilings, strip-lighting and plaster-board partitions. We are re-introducing daylight and the light-coloured, plain walls of the Regency which Smirke and the Trustees originally agreed upon. We respect the architecture as best we can, and nothing structural now done within the Museum is done without the approval of the planning authorities; nothing is irreversible. In some cases we are repairing past disasters, and this is often expensive. One in particular will have to be faced at some future date, for the PSA in an effort to economise in the 1960s laid a carpet on the marble North Staircase and fixed it by boring innumerable holes in a most untidy fashion in each riser. To restore this staircase to its original glory will cost hundreds of thousands of pounds.

But one cannot win all battles with ease. The conservation lobby, led by certain members of the Victorian Society, led a sustained and painful campaign a few years ago against the proposed redesign and redecoration of the Front Hall. By the mid-1980s the main hall of the Museum had become choked with furniture and people. A central information desk dominated the space and the direction-finding boards were executed in the style of a 1960s airport and dominated the desk: they were incidentally quite difficult to understand. Unsuitable seating compounded the muddle, and the main staircase was forbidding and hardly used. A study of the use of the hall was made by means of time-lapse photography and gradually a scheme was evolved by the Design Office which removed the dreaded central desk, provided a workable information panel for directing visitors to all parts of the Museum, an information desk, a visual barrier to the entrance to the Reading Room of the British Library and an enlarged (but more tactfully designed) bookshop in one corner.

The public, at crowded times, has to be dispersed as quickly as possible from the hall and thus direction signs had to be introduced on the walls. Lighting was the chief difficulty. The ceiling, for example, would take no chandelier as there was no central point of sufficient architectural emphasis, whilst standing-lamps were, it was agreed, too likely to clutter the floor space. Ambient light could, however, be provided by means of spot-lights hung on the small amount of wall space available and hidden behind two beams: thus the hall could be lit by pools of light and what little daylight could penetrate the few windows. To this end the pale shades preferred by Smirke were a godsend in that they lightened the hall, which had been less than tactfully decorated in blush colours some years before. The Royal Fine Arts Commission and other interested bodies were consulted and gave their approval.

Then the trouble began. One of our staff in the Prints and Drawings Department discovered a watercolour by L. W. Collman, which had been prepared for the Trustees after Robert Smirke had resigned as architect. By this time – 1847 – taste had, as mentioned before, changed and the greens, browns, ambers, blues and the gold stars of the Collman scheme were more in keeping with the taste of the mid-nineteenth century than the pale Regency colours Smirke is known to have preferred. This scheme had been executed and had survived more or less intact until the 1930s: it must have been very attractive. When the Victorian Society and the Georgian Society heard that Collman's scheme had been discovered they embarked on a campaign of vilification which ate deeply into the soul of the Museum. They claimed that they (the Victorian Society) had discovered Collman (untrue); they claimed that we had ignored Collman (untrue: when it was discovered at a very late stage of the planning process we agonised over it considerably). They produced figures which claimed that the cost of reinstating the scheme would be minimal. They estimated an overall cost of £135,000 and a period of some ten weeks to complete it once the templates for the patterns had been cut. An independent survey showed, however, that the cost of the scheme would be more in the order of £215,000 plus a possible extra £7,000 for a coat of varnish which might be necessary. Further, it was revealed that to complete this scheme the hall would have to be scaffolded out for thirty weeks, instead of the fifteen estimated for the Design Office scheme. This would take us right through the summer and our main busy period which would make visitor circulation virtually impossible.

These arguments cut no ice with the amenity societies and the planning authorities; who combined together in an attempt to stop us; and we were even threatened with prosecution if we proceeded with our scheme – something certainly not provided for in any planning act. It took nearly nine months before the planning authority grudgingly agreed that they would allow us to go ahead. We could afford neither the money nor the time to reinstate the Collman scheme; we did, however, respect the architecture in a way it had not enjoyed since the hall was first opened. We rebuilt the great plinths at the foot of the stairs and between pillars and pilasters at the front of the hall, we reintro-duced benches of Smirke's design and removed all excrescences from the main portion of the hall to give a grand feeling of space. If, at some future date, the money is available and the will is there I can see no reason why the Collman scheme should not be restored (we have done no irreversible damage in the hall), but for practical reasons that time has not yet arrived. It is strange that once the new hall was revealed in all its new glory, not a single word of criticism appeared in the press concerning it. What is more – it works! The Louvre has tackled a similar problem by building a vast glass pyramid and an underground concourse at enormous expense to cater for the difficulties of filtering a similar number of people through a similarly complicated building which had even more awkward entrances. We have not the money to indulge such a fantasy. In any case, the best way to enter a palace or a temple is up the main staircase and not by the basement entrance.

With all our faults and continuing lack of money, we cater for a vast visiting public. Surveys tell us something of that public, the press tells us a little and public comment adds to our knowledge. Surveys are notoriously unreliable, but it would seem that ap-proximately 44 per cent of our visitors are under thirty-four years of age, nearly half of these (18 per cent) may be classed as students. About half our visitors are British or Irish, of the foreign visitors 23 per cent are allegedly North American; it is interesting that the foreign language guide which sells most strongly is that translated into Japanese (38,000 per year), four times more than, for example, the French. 64 per cent of our visitors live outside

London. One of the most striking statistics of a recent survey suggests that some 60 per cent had a university degree or its equivalent, and this certainly confirms that we are right to cater for people of at least average intelligence in our labelling, information and publications. We should and do, however, make great efforts to attract a broader public. The most popular permanent exhibitions are those in the Greek and Roman and the Egyptian departments, the Rosetta Stone and the Parthenon sculptures attracting most attention. Temporary exhibitions apparently attract older visitors but few first-time visitors.

It would be dreary to continue reciting statistics, but such surveys do help us to understand the needs and criticisms of our visitors. We provide them with certain ancillary services which they seem to appreciate. The shops are particularly appreciated by foreign tourists, the restaurant by British visitors and the ice-cream kiosk by the young. The pleasure of sitting outside the Museum in the sun is only too evident, even on cold winter days. Public and school children by the score eat their sandwiches on the steps or under the portico (from September 1989 we have provided lunch space for school parties which is booked up well ahead). Week-end visits are particularly popular with the public and especially the young; at the height of summer there is standing room only in the Front Hall. Visitors also come to visit the British Library displays (Magna Carta is one of the most popular exhibits in the Museum building), but the three permanent galleries showing Library material and the Library shop are not our responsibility.

Among visitors to the Museum is a constant stream of VIPs, from Mr Gorbachev to the Prince of Wales. The British Museum is an internationally famous institution, and even in the days of jet-set diplomacy and negotiation leaders of foreign governments, ministers, generals and their wives make frequent official visits and are shown around by members of staff. Many of these important people have visited the Museum before, as students or tourists, and come again to take a break from world affairs, to be refreshed.

The collections entertain, amuse and instruct our public. We trust, however, that they are also approached with some sense of awe and wonder. Objects are treated with dignity; we try not to trivialise them and we try not to offend minorities or religious susceptibilities. We aim to provide the collections with a dignified setting so that people from all lands may experience some of the most significant objects made by man, unflustered by hype.

We are particularly conscious of the need to show the objects in context. Through information panels and the juxtaposition of the prestigious with the everyday we are able to relate the exhibits to their historical, geographical and taxonomic backgrounds. These are models which have stood the test of time: the Museum has fortunately avoided the worst excesses of structuralism, but has, particularly in its special exhibitions, attempted a more complete reconstruction of specific places, periods or cultures according to the changing fashions and demands of taste and academic thought (and prejudice), which seems to have satisfied even the Young Turks.

The Museum keeps a low profile: we are conscious that we serve a wide public and we attempt to show the collections honourably and, as befits the trust we uphold, without stridency.

Chapter 6

VALUE FOR MONEY

The Museum is largely funded by the public purse and is accountable to the public through Parliament, both for the money it spends and for the collections it holds in trust. We receive government monies in the form of grants made through our sponsor department, the Office of Arts and Libraries. The grants for 1989/90 are simply stated: £15.593m for general administrative expenses, £7.65m for building, utilities and works, and £1.4m for purchases for the collections. The total received from government is, then, £24.643m. These are the basic facts of the public commitment to the British Museum, but they hide a complicated story.

Let us first deal with the comparatively simple problem of the purchase grant. In 1985/6, without any warning, it was reduced from £1.737m to £1.4m, a level at which it has since remained. We are encouraged by the present Minister for the Arts' statement in Parliament that he intends to review the overall provision for purchase grants in 1990. I must admit to feeling ambivalent about any increase in purchase grants. A museum director's appetite for more money in this area can only be described as greedy: a museum can spend all it can get. The only museum which can be described as satiated is the Getty Museum, where £100m or more must be spent in each year.

At the beginning of the century our purchase grant was practically zero and we have been fighting for its improvement ever since. The Museum has achieved much since then but still has an ever-open maw. We could buy wisely and well in many fields given unlimited funds. But limited resources are themselves a valuable discipline, we must exercise our expertise to increase the collections – an expertise which has been emphasised throughout this book. If the Museum were allowed a grant of £2.5m (which would restore it approximately to its pre-1986 level) with access to an enhanced National Heritage Memorial Fund for the purchase of objects of national prestige and great financial value, the Trustees would be happy. The Museum would be able to enter a more satisfactory collecting phase. We need more money for the purchase of objects, but not an unreasonable amount.

However, the really serious problem concerns the money we need to pay the wages and look after the building. We have seen that the total received from government for the year 1989/90 is £24.643m. We expect to spend some £20m on general administrative expenses, £11m on buildings, utilities and works and about £2m on purchases for the collections. A total of, say, £33m. The missing £8m plus will be found in various ways. Some £2.25m will come from the recovery of costs for staff, building maintenance and utilities shared with various institutions, including the British Library. Some £640,000 comes from rents of properties owned by the Trustees. The remaining £5m we have to earn.

We have obtained gifts and bequests of over £3m towards our building expenditure, whilst our receipts from trading activities, donation boxes, entrance fees and sponsorship for special exhibitions amount to another £1m. The Trustees also have some private money as a result of donations, legacies, etc., a large proportion of which (a gift and a bequest from Mr Percy Brooke-Sewell) is reserved for the purchase of Oriental antiquities. But these funds cannot meet the projected deficit of £995,000 for the year 1989/90. This deficit will be caused by government pay policies which will be considered below.

Let us first look at the up-side of our financial position. Apart from some major expenditure of a mundane nature on services and utilities, the Museum can more or less keep its head above water on the maintenance side. New works and gallery refurbishment, however, are being carried largely by outside funding, although, rooms 70 ('Italy Before the Romans') and 71 ('Rome, City and Empire') are being refurbished from public funds (the latter with matching funding provided by the Minister for the Arts against a generous grant from the Wolfson Foundation). The new Japanese galleries, the refurbished Mesopotamian Room, and the 'Egypt in Africa' Gallery will all be funded privately in the period to 1991.

The Japanese galleries, which will open in April 1990 to display one of the best collections of Japanese arts and antiquities outside

Japan, have been funded by a concerted effort in Japan and in Britain to raise more than five million pounds towards the project. Most of this was raised in Japan with the help of the Keidanren (the Japanese equivalent of the CBI); but hefty donations from private individuals and firms – particularly Asahi Shimbun, Konica and the Urasenke Foundation – have swelled our coffers. In Britain a fund-raising team has raised a considerable sum (including a large contribution from Mr and Mrs Brian Pilkington), and the Museum itself has earned, and will earn, some hundreds of thousands of pounds towards the project through sales of replicas, a television series and a major exhibition of the treasures of the British Museum at three centres in Japan. All this could never have been achieved without the help of two friends of the Museum, Dr William Barry and his colleague, Teruko Iwanaga, a Japanese lady resident in Britain, who neglected her own business and drew on her extensive connections in Japan to perform a feat which everybody in that country deemed impossible. The work of the Japanese specialists on the Museum staff and the co-operation of all the curatorial staff in this venture has been one of the most pleasing features of my period as Director. Such fund-raising is a great strain on all concerned, but the return has been well worthwhile for Anglo-Japanese relations generally, as well as for the Museum's relations with that country.

A gift from the Raymond and Beverly Sackler Foundation, established by Dr Raymond Sackler, an American physician engaged in the pharmaceutical industry, in gratitude for Britain's public stance during Dr and Mrs Sackler's lifetime, has allowed us to start on the refurbishment of two of the upper galleries, one to redisplay the Mesopotamian collections (including the famous material from Ur) and the other gallery to contain a new display, entitled 'Egypt in Africa', which will properly exhibit for the first time our rich Nubian collections. We are at the moment engaged in the search for funding which will enable us to refurbish our Indian and Chinese galleries on the main floor of the King Edward VII Building. Here will be displayed some of the finest collections of Chinese porcelain and Indian sculpture in any museum outside their countries of origin. The public galleries in the King Edward VII Building are completed by an entirely new display of Islamic culture funded from a bequest by Sir John

Addis, a former Trustee. This exhibition includes a selection of our Iznik pottery collection, which is perhaps the best in the world and which adds a great deal of colour to the austere design of the gallery. We continue to search for funds, but it should be recognised that by the time we have finished the refurbishment and rebuilding of the public parts of the King Edwad VII Building we will have spent nearly £10m, of which more than £8m will have been raised privately.

It is not without interest that, save for a number of significant contributions from the Wolfson Foundation, most of the privately funded galleries (including the triumphant A. G. Leventis Gallery of Cypriot Antiquities) have been largely paid for out of non-British generosity. We sometimes feel that, like the prophet, the Museum is not without honour, save in its own country. It is quite clear that the reputation of the British Museum abroad is such that it is seen by many as an honour to be associated with it. Foreign firms have been particularly generous in giving us services: the Scandinavian Airline System, Royal Jordanian Airlines and Japanese Airlines, for example, have provided much free or subsidised travel. Konica have subsidised our photography, and many other firms help us in this way, impressed by the Museum's standing. The British Museum's reputation for scholarship and open-handedness is famous, and I cannot forbear from quoting a portion of the letter in which our most generous donor of recent years offered his gift:

> I should say I am motivated by my support of the Arts in general and my respect for this Institution and the people I have met there in particular. There are no political considerations. In this sense therefore it is important that you assure me the present high standards of scholarship in this department of the Museum will remain.

Gifts from British people are much rarer in recent years, although a shining exception was the bequest of Sir John Addis, mentioned above, which has enabled us to open the new Islamic gallery. This and Lord Wolfson's generosity aside, we have found it extremely difficult to raise large sums of private money in this country. Even sponsorship of exhibitions is proving more difficult as government policy drives more and more public institutions to the hard-pressed private sector for financial help. Big business is inundated by requests from all sorts of charities and, although many are generous, charities for life-and-death problems at home and abroad naturally attract more sympathy. Further, the performing arts and the fine arts seem generally to have more immediacy to the inhabitants of board-rooms than an historical museum. Business has a duty to its shareholders; many company chairmen feel that they are in business to make money for those who have invested in their work, not to give to charity. This is a totally understandable attitude, but not one that is shared by their American or Continental opposite numbers.

Patronage, as John Myerscough has recently pointed out, is really a straight donation, 'with no expectation of a direct or indirect private return'. Business sponsorship benefits the giver as well as the receiver: the sponsor gets publicity, a marketing facility or a locus for entertainment. 'In practice', he adds, 'The distinction is not always clearly observed, and many companies give to the arts for a combination of motives'. In America particularly sponsorship ($5bn, compared to £30m in Britain) is a way of life for many big companies: many belong to the 1 per cent club which gives 1 per cent of a company's net profit to charitable ends. Some companies give as much as 5 per cent. An attempt to found a similar club in this country has largely foundered.

There is a great deal to be gained by sponsorship, as has been found particularly by Olivetti in an international programme of exhibition sponsorship which is second to none in the world. The reputation of this firm throughout the world has grown on the backs of such exhibitions as *The Horses of San Marco*, *Glass of the Caesars* and the phenomenally successful 1989 exhibition of Gauguin's paintings, shared between Chicago, Washington and the Grand Palais in Paris.

No British company has yet ventured into this international field, although a few have dipped their toes tentatively in the water. The British Museum makes dozens of approaches for sponsorship to companies each year and the 'regret' letters pour in. In talking to company chairmen I find that they are embarrassed by, and sometimes impatient of, such approaches of which they may have many hundreds in the course of a year (there are signs that arts sponsorship in this country is levelling off). The British Museum does not do well in terms of exhibition sponsorship, although it is not for want of trying. Occasionally we meet a sponsor whose interest chimes with our own. British Gas sponsored *Treasures for the Nation* for the Museum and the National Heritage Memorial Fund in 1988/9; but we were unable, for example, to find a sponsor for a major exhibition on British attitudes to the French Revolution, entitled *Shadow of the Guillotine* in 1989. Prospects for future sponsorship for British Museum exhibitions look bleak, particularly as many sponsors are deterred by costs of upwards of £250,000 to mount even an average-sized exhibition with few loans.

Real money comes not so much from business sponsorship but from private patronage, from the generosity of private donors. As well as the magnificent donations made for galleries mentioned above, private gifts can and do achieve splendid ends. With great energy one of our Assistant Keepers has collected a significant sum towards a colourful exhibition at the Museum of Mankind entitled *Palestinian Costume*. She raised the money by personal appeal to institutions and individuals with connections in the Middle East, both British and foreign. A Hong Kong businessman has generously promised to fund an exchange programme of curators and conservators with China, whilst an American with interests in Indian antiquities is funding the preparation of a major catalogue of Gandharan sculpture by providing for the employment of a replacement to release our specialist in this subject from day-to-day departmental duties.

One aspect of private generosity is shown through the British Museum Society. Founded as a 'supporters' club', its members have many privileges but also provide the Museum with cash for projects as diverse as a successful series of field trips to Madagascar, the purchase of contemporary works on paper, the fitting out of a store-room and so on. Recently the Society has acted as a medium through which we have recruited over sixty patrons at £1,000 per year and a number of associates at £100. If we can develop this useful body we may in, in future, be able to count on a substantial income from this source. Even in small private giving there are many difficulties. In Britain the social and medical charities will always win out. Changing attitudes of mind to the serious support by individuals of the arts and academic charities is going to be hard work (to the extent, say, of 1 per cent of net salary): the country's philanthropic culture will have to be altered through education. The American experience in this area is a spur, but it cannot easily be transplated here; we must, however, try.

The problem of raising money in an increasingly competitive world cannot be underestimated. It is one of the most difficult, nail-biting jobs. When it works it is marvellous, but the refusals are many and sometimes quite brusque. There are many false dawns; many hopeful, probing lunches and much wasted time and effort. The strain of travelling, of entertaining, of being entertained and of using social connections is part of the lot of a modern museum director. The job changes with the times – and the going can be pretty rough – but the rewards are great in terms of contacts made and problems shared. The almost universal goodwill towards the Museum, particularly abroad, relieves the pain and the shame of the begging bowl.

Generally, however, we cannot raise significant financial help towards our running costs. We have yet to see warders with sponsorship labels on their jackets! The largest element in the Museum's running costs is staff pay and superannuation. We are a highly labour-intensive institution. In 1981 and the following years government ceased completely to fund full costs of the pay awards which they made (fig. 3). In previous years supplementary votes were available to meet the bill for pay awards which were in excess of our original provision based on the Public Expenditure Survey. In 1981 the Vote for our general administrative expenditure amounted to £1m over our salary bill. In 1989 it was £1m less than our salary bill. In general, our government funding has increased between 3 per cent and 4 per cent while some pay awards, decided by central government with no adequate advisory input from Non-Departmental Public Bodies, have topped 7 per cent. We have only been able to keep paying our salaries by savage cuts in staff numbers, by keeping posts vacant (we have about 150 such vacancies at present), by private fund-raising and by earning extra monies. The cuts have been bearable but cumulative, and we have now reached the heel of the salami. The restructuring of salary scales, the introduction of performance pay and London weighting have far outstripped our ability to pay. The Treasury, which sets the awards at the levels they feel necessary for the whole Civil Service, say that it is up to sponsor departments to battle for extra funds. But our sponsor department has been unable to deliver because of heavy calls elsewhere

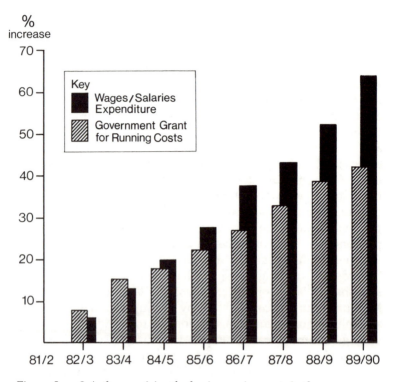

%
increase

Key
■ Wages/Salaries Expenditure
▨ Government Grant for Running Costs

Fig. 3. In 1981/2 the provision for basic running costs in the government vote for the British Museum was £9.424m and pay expenditure was £8.770m. The comparative figures for 1989/90 on the same baseline are £13.471m and £14.619m.

on the arts budget. Although it is true that funding for museums has increased in real terms since 1981, this is largely taken up by extra money (some 3.6m in the 1987/8 budget) for the Museums and Galleries Commission and by some £12.5m replacement funding for institutions left homeless after the abolition of the GLC and the other metropolitan boroughs (fig. 4). In addition, since 1980/1 the funding of the National Heritage Memorial Fund and the process of acceptance in lieu of Capital Gains Tax had by 1987/8 added another £9.1m to the annual bill.

The standard text-book, *How to lie with Statistics*, is by every civil servant's and every museum director's bedside; but, whatever is said, it is impossible to get away from the fact that museum salaries have been underfunded for years and that the practice

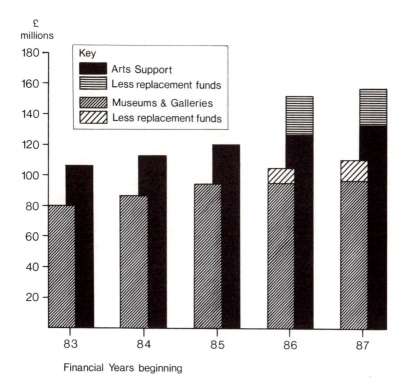

£
millions

Key
- ■ Arts Support
- ☰ Less replacement funds
- ▨ Museums & Galleries
- ▧ Less replacement funds

83   84   85   86   87

Financial Years beginning

Fig. 4. The abolition of the metropolitan boroughs in 1985 led to a large rise in the government's financial support for the arts as replacement funds were found centrally. The underlying rise in expenditure on museums and galleries has, however, not been so dramatic. (Source: Policy Studies Institute, *Cultural Trends 1989*)

must now cease or museums must change character completely. The cause of our first ever budgeted deficit of £995,000 for 1989/90 is the result of an exceptionally heavy series of pay awards and salary restructuring. (Restructuring, salary awards and allowances in one grade in the eighteen months from April 1989 will increase by more than 25 per cent – our allowance from government for this, unless we receive supplementary money, will be only about a fifth of the sum we will be obliged to pay.) We have told the Office of Arts and Libraries that we cannot afford new performance pay, which is in many cases inappropriate to our circumstances, and have pleaded for a grant from the Contingency Fund to match normal pay awards: we now wait despairingly for a reply. What is more, this is not a one-off call for support; it is necessary to raise the base-line and index it in future years to the level of pay awards.

Lurking at the back of our minds is the suspicion that the Treasury wishes to break the staff's parity with the main-line Civil Service grades; a parity which was gradually achieved over the post-War years and culminated in the Couzens–Hayward agreement (see pp. 59f.). The advantage, according to current Government dogma, of breaking the link is that we would be able to go into the market-place and buy better managers. What is left unsaid is that other salaries would have to be reduced in order to prop up the enhanced salaries of the experts brought in to govern us. Even if we were to do this, we would have to create redundancies and pay for them, reduce current salary levels, or let the reductions work through the system over the next generation (we have a remarkably stable staff, whose careers tend to be museum-orientated). Breaking this parity would require legislation and in fairness we question its necessity. It would also be hideously expensive, and we have, in any case, sufficient flexibility within our present grading structure to pay anybody at an appropriate rate.

Members of staff with both Civil Service and academic backgrounds are quite capable of moving within the present managerial parameters of the Museum. There is every reason why a Director should be an academic, in exactly the same way that a Vice-Chancellor should be an academic (and there are a good many more of them). Despite all the committees and consultants who have crawled over the Museum in the last few years, the British Museum has not been taken to task for any major managerial failure. There is a tendency for critics nowadays to say, 'the present system must be bad, do something; we don't care what you do, but do something'. I believe that the traditional values of the tightened-up management of the British Museum serve the Nation and the international community well. We do not need a lot of extra money, but full funding of salary awards (awards over which we have no control) would ensure that we could continue to provide all the services demanded of us and move with the times by fine-tuning of our existing organisation, instead of making savings through the accidents of wastage because of retirement or death.

But then it is asked, 'why not charge for entry?' – as if this would solve all our ills. Charging this year might allow us to meet this year's threatened deficit on our wages bill, but we have no guarantee that our grant would not be eroded as a result of generating a predictable level of income. It is noticeable that those national museums which charge for entry are just as anxious to have their salary bills met by Treasury as those which do not; the percentage of the running costs raised is very small. Even if we did charge for entry we calculate that by the early 1990s all financial advantage would be eroded if there was no change in government policy on funding salary awards.

Arguments for charging will always be offered – the first such suggestions were indeed made in 1793 – and rejected on the grounds that the revenue so raised 'would bear but a small proportion to the deficiencies of the regular expenditure of the Museum'. In 1929 an earlier Director, Sir Frederic Kenyon, in a memorandum submitted to Royal Commission on the National Museums and Galleries stated robustly:

> The question at issue is a very simple one. Is it desired to encourage the use of the museum or is it not? There is not the smallest doubt that the imposition of fees discourages attendances . . . The question, therefore, simply is whether it is worth while to exclude the public (and especially, of course, the poorer members of the public) for the sake of the pecuniary return to be expected from fees . . . The nation has a very large capital invested in the Museum, and it is better to look for the return on it from the educational advantages offered to the public, than from a trivial taking of cash at the turnstiles.

What was stated then is as true today. 1929 was not the happiest of years economically, and if the government of that period could eschew charging, how much more should not the government of the prosperous 1980s?

Economic arguments should not always rule. The philosophy of the Museum (as enshrined in its Act and in the intention of its founding Trustees) is to make the Museum as available as possible to the interested public, and this stance has been held consistently by both staff and Trustees since 1753. Arguments against charging, therefore, permeate the whole ethos of our thinking. And not only ours: most of the national museums and galleries in this country have set their face against charging, as have many national museums abroad, although not now sadly in Latin Europe. The great museums of the Preussischer Kultur-besitz in Berlin are free, as are all the federal museums and galleries in Washington and the national museums of Denmark and Norway. Many of the other major museums in these countries also do not charge for entry – the great, newly redesigned Staatsgallerie in Stuttgart, for example. Great Britain pioneered free entry to museums; we should be proud of this fact and should, for many reasons, not attempt to deny this great imaginative tradition.

Further, there is a good practical reason for not charging. Many people visit the Museum for very short periods, to see a favourite object or examine something which has caught their eye. They slip in between meetings, in the lunch hour, before appointments, to get out of the rain, or because they happen to be passing. They do not spend hours wandering round miles of galleries. In many respects this is the most splendid way to enjoy a museum, one which the habitual museum-goer uses all the time. If the Museum were to charge we would lose many of these casual and most appreciative of visitors – particularly the lower paid, of whom there are a great many in Bloomsbury – who would be deterred by a charge for a few minutes' contemplation.

But the arguments against charging are not based simply on the philosophy of free access to the collections. There are two very potent arguments for such free access: first, that charging undoubtedly greatly reduces the number of visitors to an institution, and, second, that the amount of money raised by charging would not significantly add to the income of the Museum. If cost-effectiveness is an index of the value of the Museum the former is a strong argument.

It cannot be denied that charging for entry means a drop in the number of visitors. This was clearly shown when all national museums were required by government to charge, a procedure which lasted for about three months in 1974. At that time visitors to the British Museum dropped by 60 per cent. Non-official figures suggest that in the first three months of charging in 1988 visitor numbers at the Science Museum dropped by more than 50 per cent. The period involved in both cases was very short and it could be wrong to make statistical mileage from such unrepresentative figures. What can be gauged more accurately is the effect on visitor numbers at the Victoria and Albert Museum since the introduction of a voluntary charging system in November 1985. In the final full year of free access visitor numbers stood at 2.079m; in 1988 they had sunk to 1.43m, a fall of 31 per cent. This is shown graphically against the British Museum's figures, which have risen by about 20 per cent since that date. The scale of the effect of charging on visitor numbers is undeniable. The cost for each visitor to the British Museum, set against the total government grant (including purchase grant) for the financial year 1988/9, is £5.65 – which is not expensive. If we were to charge, the cost per head would increase appreciably.

And so we come to the question of how much money would be raised by charging. We have done various projections, which are shown in the table on p. 102. We are, however, conscious that such forecasting may be compared to star-gazing. The awful warning of the Victoria and Albert Museum, which estimated that it would make £500,000 from voluntary contributors in its first year of charging and actually produced less than half of that sum – £222,723 (gross = £400,000) is ever present. It is accepted that in the first year at least a decrease of some 40 per cent in visitor numbers would result from museum charges. I give this comparatively low figure because it is possible that the British Museum might not suffer quite so much as other museums as it has a very high proportion of tourists. However, it would be unwise to assume that losses of revenue from British visitors deterred by an admission charge would invariably be made up by that received from foreign tourists. The tourist trade is notoriously susceptible to external events, as can be seen by the decrease of some 25 per cent in the tourist attendance at the British Museum (and a comparable fall in shop revenue) for a few months following the American bombing of Libya.

The logistics of charging would be considerable: erecting ticketing machines in the already inadequate entrance of a Grade I listed building, for example, is not the simplest of processes; turnstiles would generate long queues (particularly at weekends); coping with people who use the building for non-Museum business (e.g. British Library readers) would cause further difficulties, and so would the drawing up of an agreement on a fair distribution of the profit with the British Library itself. These and many more problems – which range from VAT to school parties –

would have to be taken into account. All, however, could be overcome and charges introduced. In order to compile realistic figures we should first reduce the actual published number of visitors at Bloomsbury to 3m (this allows for British Library readers, visitors on official business and the visitors at the Museum of Mankind where charging would certainly not be

Average annual attendance

Free	500,000
Full rate	2,000,000
Reduced rate	1,000,000
Total	3,500,000

	a. 50p/£1	b. £1/£2	c. £2 annual
Fall in attendance	25%	35%	25%
Projected revenue	£	£	£
Paying visitors: full	1,500,000	1,300,000	2,250,000
concessions	750,000	650,000	nil
Gross revenue from ticket sales	1,875,000	3,250,000	4,500,000
Total revenue after deducting VAT	**1,630,000**	**2,827,000**	**3,913,000**
Deductions	£	£	£
Staff	275,000	275,000	120,000
Maintenance	6,000	6,000	6,000
Tickets	5,000	5,000	5,000
Warders for galleries	150,000	150,000	150,000
Equipment and alterations	260,000	260,000	260,000
Total deductions	**696,000**	**696,000**	**541,000**
Net revenue	934,000	2,131,000	3,372,000
7% to British Library	65,000	149,000	236,000
Total income	**869,000**	**1,982,000**	**3,136,000**

Fig. 5
Estimated calculations of income from admission charges at Bloomsbury after three years.

economically viable as so few people find their way there), so that the table presents three possible scenarios.

These figures are the sort we would expect to see in the fourth year after the introduction of charges. They are rather optimistic, but assume that there would be some recovery from an initial, fairly disastrous (if we were to follow the example of the Science Museum), fall in visitors. At best charges would produce 9 per cent of the total costs of running the Museum, at worst 3 per cent.

On the debit side we would clearly lose some of our present receipts: a sum in many ways difficult to quantify. We would lose about £100,000 annually in voluntary donations through our collecting boxes. We would probably have to cease charging for temporary exhibitions, which could lose us £150,000 each year and probably more. We would certainly lose turnover in our shops and restaurants, which in the case of the former might make the difference between profitability and loss, and in the case of the latter might cause problems with the licensee, because margins would be reduced.

In financial terms the rewards seem minimal and would soon be eroded, either by the continuation of the present policy of underfunding salaries, or by the normal machinations of a Treasury which has for years in effect said, 'they can always afford to cut a little more'. We would also lose a lot of public goodwill, some of which might not be recovered. Anecdotally, it is interesting that after four years of voluntary charging at the Victoria and Albert Museum, people still tell me that they will not darken its doors again because they disapprove so strongly of the new policy; it is also clear that the Victoria and Albert Museum has lost a lot of its traditional support in London and the Home Counties. It is probable that the increase in visitors to the British Museum, the National Gallery and the Tate, in contrast to the trend over the last few years, may well be a result of the charging policies of the South Kensington group of museums sending visitors elsewhere.

There is, however, a firm moral base for not charging, a base which is non-financial and which explains why Trustees and staff have backed free access on innumerable occasions since the spectre was first raised in the late eighteenth century. The ideal of free admission has been defended long and honourably by the British public: it has certainly been central to the thinking of many of the Museum's benefactors. Is it worth saving a minimal amount of money to deny access to more than a million people annually? I could not morally accept such a decision.

The British Museum is a nationally and internationally loved institution; it should (and does) offer a wide experience to an audience uncircumscribed by nationality, age, wealth, class, background or intellectual capacity. The Museum should be freely available to everyone, to stretch minds, stimulate their curiosity and provide for their academic needs. The Trustees hold the collections in trust for the nation and for the world, and have done so for centuries; it is a sign of a civilised society to make these collections as widely available as possible. The taxpayer pays for the Museum; the taxpayer should, therefore, be allowed to see it without charge. Nor should we discriminate against tourists (who contribute greatly to the invisible earnings of this country), particularly as so many of those who come to the Museum are young and, like most young, are impoverished. The fact that we hold so many foreign treasures in the institution means that we have a moral responsibility to place as few barriers as possible between nationals of that or any other country who wish to see them. There are some services which a proud and civilised nation should provide free: the British Museum, cherished in this tradition for nearly two and a half centuries, is surely one of these. Britain should be proud to hold such an institution in trust for all time in the spirit enunciated by its founding trustees and defended so vigorously through so many vicissitudes. As we increase our income by commercial means, as generous donors provide major sums for capital expenditure and individuals help by giving smaller sums to make the Museum more attractive, as the Trustees manage their investments, as the average visitor puts more money into our donation boxes, so perhaps taxpayer and government can afford what is, to them, a petty sum to allow us to continue not to charge for entry. We have worked hard to achieve our present financial equilibrium and continue to work hard to maintain it; we are, however, really threatened with trouble. We trust that government will help us with the necessary financial assistance which will enable us to continue to provide a free and wide-ranging service to our public, both popular and academic.

The British Museum is by no means bankrupt, but unless

government recognises that we need greater support we shall soon be in serious deficit. A small touch to windward on the tiller of government expenditure would see us well into the 1990s.

Chapter 7

A MUSEUM FOR ALL NATIONS

No cultural museum in the world is so international in its activities as the British Museum. Only great science-based museums, like the Smithsonian Institution in Washington, challenge in breadth its interests. The British Museum provides a popular spectacle for visitors from every country in the world (some 50 per cent of its visitors coming from abroad) and it is a Mecca for scholars in all branches of cultural history and art. It answers queries from all over the world at all levels of scholarship, from the intricate details of scholarly nit-picking, to general appeals for knowledge from the non-academic who seeks an opinion at the highest level. The various departments collaborate in international projects of research, excavation, indexing and field collecting. It is by far the most accessible and welcoming of the major collections, not only to scholars, but also to younger students and to interested amateurs from all over the world. Its staff travels widely, studying, consulting, excavating, lecturing, accompanying loans, collaborating in publishing projects, advising on conservation, fund-raising and representing Britain on international committees. We also have our international problems: everybody has heard of the Elgin Marbles!

The international functions of the institution go largely unrecognised in this country and it was unfortunate that when the House of Commons Foreign Affairs Committee recently examined the Museum on its role in cultural diplomacy it did not have the time, because of the 1987 General Election, to comment on the evidence given by the Museum. Sometimes we do not ourselves realise the importance of our international standing. Even the French, who from the time of Napoleon onwards have believed that all culture begins and ends in France, acknowledge the quality of only one foreign institution – one that is affectionately named 'le British'! Although the Museum is the most important of this country's museums in the eyes of the world, our other national museums are also looked at with great respect; the complicated and much publicised events of the Victoria and Albert Museum in early 1989, for example, were anxiously discussed abroad, both privately among professionals and in the press.

Senior colleagues in local museums in America tell me in emphatic terms that the vast majority of American museum administrators look towards Britain for help, and use our institutions as models of how a museum or gallery should be organised; they consider the British Museum as the most important representative of this group and they are worried by some of the current museum trends in our country, for they also have been through many of the traumas of cut-backs and reorganisation that seem to threaten us. They tell me that, where we once led the world, the British are beginning to appear provincial and that respect for our expertise is on the wane. They point to France (where about 8,000m francs – about £800m – are to be spent on reorganising the Louvre alone), where new and refurbished museums and buildings are eagerly funded by the state, and to which country they turn more and more frequently for collaboration in major exhibitions. They still see the British Museum as a bastion of international co-operation but worry for us, perhaps unreasonably. Probably, they say, because the British Museum has not got the glamour and high profile of an art museum and because of the strength of our collections, we stand a better chance of survival as a centre of international excellence. I dislike the word 'probably'; the Museum will do all it can to retain that excellence. This view from America recognises our international status, but points the problem.

An important element in the Museum's international activities concerns loans to foreign institutions. In 1985 we lent 695 objects, valued at £32.1m, to 47 centres in 12 countries (chiefly the United States); in 1988 we lent 646 objects, valued at £30.3m, to 65 centres in 15 countries. The staff of the Museum willingly collaborate with their colleagues abroad, both in the production of catalogues and in the organisation of the displays themselves. But foreign loans throw a considerable charge on the Museum's resources, particularly as in many cases it is to the British Museum, with its comprehensive, well-organised and well-catalogued collections, that organisers of exhibitions turn first. Whilst recouping expenses for photographs, transport, packing and courier subsistence, the Museum does not normally – save in the case of large loans – charge for conservation, curatorial and administrative time. We have considered doing so, but on a practical front the administrative problems of making even a standard charge would be out of proportion to the return we might get. Further, we consider it our duty, as we hold the objects in trust, that we should make our collections as freely available as possible and any charge might deter borrowers. We thus follow the normally accepted practice in most countries. In certain cases, when very considerable loans are made, we have received reasonable financial return for our efforts. Sometimes the return is less clearly seen: because we made a major loan of Ukiyoe prints to Japan, the sponsors of the exhibition, the newspaper *Asahi Shimbun*, became one of our principal sponsors and supporters in our Japanese fund-raising.

There has been a marked decrease in the number of foreign loans in recent years, partly due to the increasing cost of mounting international exhibitions. It also, however, reflects the gradual erosion of the Museum's financial resources in the 1980s. For the first time we have had to refuse loan requests due to lack of staff. It should be emphasised that all the exhibitions to which we lend abroad have an academic basis: the exhibition catalogues become standard works of reference; thus parts of our collection are set in context and become more accessible academically. We try not to lend to frivolous exhibitions which are merely eye-catching and tell no story. Great international exhibitions have become very big business indeed; sophisticated methods of transport have made them more easily realisable. Much political kudos is to be gained by both the borrowing and lending countries through such loans, and the Museum at times must tread a difficult political tightrope across yawning spaces of diplomatic pressure, internal politics, financial blandishments and simple self-interest, before deciding whether to borrow or lend. Every year we turn down many requests for loans; such decisions are not always popular either at home or abroad. Financial constraints are not the only reason for the refusal of loans. Most of the refusals are the result of adverse conservation or security reports:

borrowers and lenders are only too aware that damage can result from transporting objects. To an extent all items which are loaned live dangerously; one day something unique and famous will fall out of the sky. This risk must be accepted and, when it happens, lending museums must try not to close down international exhibitions for all time. Such shows have an enormous and increasingly important significance both in academic terms and in so far as they increase international understanding and goodwill. They also make good sense economically: the French have long realised that trade follows culture.

The Museum itself borrows from foreign institutions, sometimes whole exhibitions. Since 1980 we have had eighteen loan exhibitions from abroad. The Museum set the fashion for great 'blockbuster' exhibitions; the first was the Tutankhamun exhibition in 1972 which had 1.7m visitors. But, as sponsors get more difficult to tempt into our net, and as we have to count the cost of travel so carefully, we must inevitably be thrown back on our own considerable resources and collections. We still borrow items – sparingly – for exhibitions we initiate ourselves. I hope this will not become an increasingly rare event in the future. Collaboration with a good sponsor, as with Olivetti on the *Glass of the Caesars* exhibition (and, in this case, co-operation with other contributing museums, Corning in New York State and Cologne), can work wonders. We have not given up such shows, as the Kamakura exhibition (a study of brilliant medieval Japanese sculpture) planned for 1991 will show.

The Department of Ethnography has been remarkably successful in gaining support for exhibitions from indigenous peoples and from people of goodwill in the countries whence the objects come. A large sum of money was raised in Canada for the *Living Arctic* exhibition, and the same as we have seen is true of the *Palestinian Costume* exhibition which opened in 1989: both exhibit the measure of support the Museum receives from friends abroad.

Co-operative work in collecting, particularly in the Third World, has benefited both the Museum and the countries in which the collections have been made. Such benefits come in a number of ways. As we increase our collections and our knowledge of their cultures so we increase their knowledge and help them. Bringing foreign colleagues to the British Museum, we learn from them and train them in our techniques. We also help them document their collections and often suggest future projects. And we are helping to preserve a record of the material culture of the ordinary people of, for example, Mali or Guinea Bissau, Bolivia or Mexico, the Sudan or Gujarat, thus increasing an understanding of these people, but also ensuring that their culture will be available for comparative study in London.

An example of such work may be illustrated by a project based in Madagascar. Financed in part by the British Museum Society, the Museum collaborated with Malagasy colleagues, collecting, recording, photographing and dividing the collections. When brought to England much of the material was mounted as a popular exhibition. This was opened in 1986 by a group of ministers of the Malagasy government, who had come here especially for that purpose. The political and diplomatic goodwill engendered by this expedition and the subsequent exhibition in London and New York was considerable.

Collecting archaeological material abroad is more difficult than in earlier periods. Here we rely on official *partage* (the division of finds after excavation). In some countries, Jordan for example, this may be very generous; in others less so. But often a handful of sherds from a cultural context will illuminate collections made on a much grander scale in the last century. The goodwill engendered by our participation in excavations even when there is no *partage* is of considerable political value. We were, for example, working in Iraq for most seasons during the Gulf War and consequently enjoy excellent relations with our colleagues there. Our work in collaboration with University College London and the University of Peshawar on the Bannu Archaeological Project has created immense interest and goodwill in Pakistan in a sometimes awkward political climate.

Co-operative collecting can also take place in non-archaeological areas. A remarkable example of enlightened self-interest on both British and Czechoslovak sides was the exchange of prints collected specifically to illustrate the art of these two countries in the last hundred years. Czechoslovak prints from an extremely interesting period were given to the British Museum and displayed here. A similar gift and exhibition was arranged by us for the National Gallery in Prague through the British Museum Society.

I have stressed the international character of the scholars who use our collections. International co-operation with the Department of Conservation is also considerable; in the last few years we have accepted conservation trainees from as far away as Japan and Australia. A recent secondment from the Shanghai Museum of a Chinese paper conservation specialist has proved of great mutual benefit, keeping alive a long-standing relationship between the two institutions. In the field of education we welcome seconded teachers from countries who help us with current exhibitions. An education officer from the Royal Ontario Museum, funded by a private bursary, recently spent six months observing our work and helping it in relation to the *Living Arctic* exhibition. The Design Office is much consulted by foreign museums from Hawaii to Poland, and we have welcomed designers on long-term attachment: for example, from Brunei.

Our curatorial contacts are vast. Curators from the Cairo Museum have spent extended periods in the Egyptian Department and such secondments are frequently made to the Department of Ethnography. Exchanges like these provide us with willing academic collaboration and also much-needed primary help in areas where we are short-staffed: both sides gain. Curators and other members of staff frequently advise foreign countries on the setting up of projects or museums: they give advice on conservation to the Maldive Islands and on computer records for the Indira Gandhi Centre; sit on a jury in Japan to select works for an exhibition of Japanese prints for world-wide display, and advise the Indian High Commission in a long-running legal case concerning the illegal export of a major sculpture.

There is no system of sabbatical leave in the Museum. On the other hand, the staff travel frequently and sometimes for extended periods. The Keeper of Egyptian Antiquities, for example, recently spent a year as Professor at Heidelberg University, and a Deputy Keeper in the Department of Coins and Medals held a visiting fellowship for a year at the American Numismatic Society to enable him to complete his definitive catalogue on the coins of Alexander the Great. Although such long periods of secondment are rare, long-term international projects of academic collaboration on specific projects are more common: one member of staff, for example, works with Harvard University to publish the Sackler collection of Chinese bronzes, and many work on the great international corpora of material, such as Etruscan mirrors. All this goes on alongside a round of international lectures, seminars and committees (the Museum is represented on the committees or councils of more than thirty international organisations).

In all joint ventures with foreign institutions we work closely with the British Council, the British Academy, the Foreign and Commonwealth Office, the British Schools of Archaeology abroad and with British diplomats on the ground in foreign countries. We are often a bright element in countries with which relations are otherwise strained (in Madagascar we were the first Western institution to carry out research after a virtual close-down in diplomatic contact); we are often working in areas where British influence, once strong, is declining and where the name of the British Museum opens doors closed to many others. As Director of the Museum, I receive a multitude of international invitations to travel, consult and lecture, many of which I have, with great reluctance, to turn down. I ration such travel severely and am rarely away from the Museum for more than five days at a time, but the invitations I receive are a measure of the respect we are held in throughout the world.

Our main difficulties lie in our very internationality. Under-standably, some countries seeing objects from their own past in the British Museum, and in many other museums in the world, campaign for their return. This fuels cultural chauvinism which sometimes sparks portmanteau demands for the 'restitution' of cultural material to its homeland. Such demands were particu-larly virulent just before the United Kingdom and the United States left UNESCO; they are not so common at present, but will undoubtedly reappear on the international cultural agenda. Views on restitution are held with passion and genuine feeling by some people in this country, who see the collections of the Museum as anachronistic relics of a colonial past. The feeling of the nationals of the countries whose objects we hold is by no means uniform and is often ambivalent. Most are delighted that their own culture is displayed or available for study in one of the greatest museums in the world – often uniquely in relation to the material culture of other nations or regions and our collections are seen as ambassadors for their own culture. Most museum profes-sionals take this view, as do many politicians.

Occasionally, however, sectarian or political considerations surface which result in campaigns to return objects. A Benin ivory mask, for example, was adopted as the emblem of a pan-African arts festival held in Nigeria in 1976. The festival organisers wanted to borrow the mask which belongs to the British Museum, but on conservation grounds – the great delicacy, fragility and instability of the object – it was decided that it would have put the mask too much at risk if it were allowed to travel. The Museum had to refuse the loan, but offered to make a replica for presentation to the festival. This led to an extraordinary outburst of anti-colonial feeling. We were berated by the organisers of the festival, by Nigerian politicians, by expatriate African artists in London; we were summoned to see the Foreign Secretary and for a period of six months all hell broke loose. In vain we pointed out that our mask was one of four, that one of the other three had been sold on the open market to the Museum of Modern Art in New York some years earlier and that another was still in private hands and might have been available for purchase. We also pointed out that the British Museum had been instrumental in establishing the Nigerian National Museum and had steered many Benin objects from London to Lagos. All to no avail; unthinking columnists in this country and abroad accused us of colonial chauvinism and asked why we could not return this single item to its country of origin. No more has been heard of this demand since, and our relations with our professional colleagues in Nigeria remain warm.

Not long after this, in 1980, a demand came from a Minister of State of a particular ex-colonial country, who asked for the return of all the objects in the possession of the British Museum which came from that country; he enclosed a complete list. (The said minister had studied this material for his PhD in London and had compiled his list from our records.) We were rather nonplussed by the request as much of the material was similar to that available in great quantity and superior quality among the collections of the museums and public buildings of his own country and, while we do have one remarkable piece from this country upon which envious eyes had been cast in the past, we wondered why this demand had been made. We were even more puzzled as about a month later we received through official channels a significant gift of archaeological material from that country from an excavation which we had partly financed. After amicable discussion the demand was withdrawn.

The present long-running soap-opera regarding the Elgin Marbles was also fuelled politically although there is genuine feeling among a vociferous, but comparatively small group of philhellenes in this country and among certain nationalistic elements in Greece that the Parthenon marbles should be returned. Strangely enough, before that powerful, courageous and charismatic figure, Melina Mercouri, became Minister of Culture in Greece in 1981 there had been few demands for the return of the marbles. We have some folk tradition of a demand in the late 1920s, but of this there is no documentation, although there was apparently an extraordinary wartime episode when Winston Churchill casually suggested that the marbles should be returned to Greece as a gesture of allied solidarity (no more was ever heard of this flight of fancy). Everything was quiet: British and Greek archaeologists worked closely and harmoniously together and indeed a few months before the accession of Miss Mercouri to her ministerial position, I was invited to write a survey on the archaeological museums and monuments service of Greece for her predecessor. At that time not a single politician or archaeologist that I came across raised the problem of the Marbles; in fact, all admired the way in which we had displayed them in London and referred happily and constantly to the *fait accompli*. A few months later we were fighting a difficult and dirty battle in the press (although it was very noticeable that our archaeological colleagues kept a very low profile). Madame Mercouri paid a much publicised visit to the Museum in the presence of the world's press and much was said on both sides some of which was distorted or misrepresented by the media. At the moment the matter is quiescent, but there are occasional rumblings. A postal 'campaign' for the return of the marbles was mounted in early 1989, but all the letters were traced back to five or six addresses in New York, many of them even addressed by the same hand.

What is our position on the marbles? The architectural sculptures removed from the Parthenon in the early nineteenth century by Lord Elgin and his agents, with full permission from the then appropriate authorities, were purchased from him by the British Government in 1816 and entrusted to the British Museum 'to be preserved and kept together'. They have been displayed to the public ever since (save for evacuation during the Second World War) and indeed did much to change European taste for classical art and to encourage a support for the then emerging Greek nation. Up to the time of Elgin English and Continental taste for classical art was based on Roman antiquities. The Greek revival began in part with the introduction of the Elgin Marbles to the educated public of Western Europe. The romanticism of such philhellenes as Lord Byron encouraged the Greek taste, although Byron himself had a personal grudge against Elgin and no particular liking for the marbles:

> Noseless himself, he brings home noseless blocks
> To show at once the ravages of time and pox.

The Parthenon sculptures were housed in a gallery which was purpose-built and is scientifically equipped to maintain a constantly correct environment for their presentation. They are well labelled and the lighting which enhances their beauty won a national award from the industry in 1988. The only controversy that has ever concerned the condition of the sculptures was an unfinished attempt to clean them in the late 1930s. This caused a stir in the press at the time and is still occasionally referred to by critics. This action was completely in tune with contemporary conservation practices and may be compared with Kenneth Clark's programme of picture-cleaning in the National Gallery, which was similarly controversial. Visitors can judge the results for themselves when they look at the cleaned and uncleaned elements today.

There are a number of reasons why we cannot contemplate the return of any part of our collections to the country of origin. It should, however, be emphasised that local conditions – whether of security, atmospheric pollution, political instability or even past history – are not among them. Nor do we hide completely behind our Act of Parliament, because Acts of Parliament can be repealed or amended. Rather we defend our retention on good philosophical grounds. The Museum was founded as a universal museum and has remained true to the ideas of its founders to this day. It is designed to present as complete and integrated a picture as possible of the development of different but related cultures through the ages. The establishment of the Museum as a trust with a board of trustees was surely intended to inhibit political, emotional, nationalistic or sentimental influence on the collections held in trust. I have shown how, when trusts are occasionally broken and material disposed of, the institution often ultimately regrets the decision. Our argument is not the childish idea expressed in the words, 'It's mine', rather it is the sense of curatorial responsibility, of holding material in trust for mankind throughout the foreseeable future.

The British Museum, as I have emphasised, is a considerable element in the cultural heritage of the world; to start to dismantle it by bowing to unthinking, if understandable, nationalistic demands would be to start a process of cultural vandalism which would make the politicisation of art in the 1930s in Germany look like a petulant child's destruction of its dinner. In the course of this book I have tried to stress the unique quality of the Museum in international terms; if one domino falls, the rest will surely follow. If the British Museum is the first to give in, the other great museums of the world would be under pressure to follow suit and the spirit of man would be the poorer. In a period when all our aspirations are based on the hopes of international agreement, we cannot let narrow nationalism destroy a trust for the whole world. Great Britain cannot afford to deny the trust so wisely established in 1753.

But, it is sometimes argued, most of the Museum's collections were acquired through acts of dubious legality. They were pillaged, bought for the equivalent of a mess of pottage, stolen or ripped from their context without care or thought. History, however, moves on: laws change; views of morality are altered. What is pillage in the twentieth century was seen as a highly civilised and legal process in the eighteenth century. There are disgraceful episodes of which nobody can be proud. We have, for example, in the great Waddesdon Bequest the reliquary of the Holy Thorn from the Treasury in Vienna; this had been sent out for cleaning and repair in the mid-nineteenth century but was copied by the jeweller, who sent the copy to the Treasury and sold the original in the open market. The reliquary of the head of St Eustace was sold by the state over the head of the Church in Basel at the time of the secularisation (the Musée de Cluny in Paris has an altar from the same sale). Nobody asks us to return these objects, nor should they. What is sauce for the goose is sauce for the gander: the questionable legality of the sale of

Charles I's great painting collection does not mean that we should sue half the world's great art museums for its return. However much museum professionals distance themselves from dealers, they must do business with them, and we hope that the example set by the responsible museums in the world that they should never buy important things of dubious provenance should be universally followed. The British Museum certainly always asks the question of provenance before it buys and always rejects objects for which there could be the slightest question of illegality. We have missed some great treasures in that fashion, but we have also, by the same token built up great international standing through honest dealing.

Britain rightly tries to protect its own heritage. The British Museum plays a major role in this process, but not everything can be kept in this country; after all, Britain is a centre of the international art market (objects to the value of £1,286,676,000 exported in 1987/8). Some things must be protected at all costs, but it is good to see English art abroad; a Henry Moore, a Sickert, a Gainsborough are enhanced when seen in the same building as Benjamin West, Mondrian and Poussin. Our history, our art, our culture are seen in a wider context.

Chapter 8

WHERE DO WE GO FROM HERE?

At few periods in its history has the British Museum been in a position of such hope and at the same time such anxiety. Within the period up to 1996 the Museum must tackle its biggest physical change since the 1880s. As the British Library moves out, so the Museum has an opportunity to expand its exhibition space, get rid of outstations, create new displays and storage, and make manning more logical and therefore more efficient. Between then and now a new Director has to be chosen and the staff set, through consultation, to construct a completely revamped Museum for the next century. This is the element of hope and challenge.

In a period of greater sophistication in the entertainment industry, of high investment in the arts, it is argued that the customer must be appeased with 'exciting' and 'more relevant' museums – closer perhaps to theme parks – and that the head of such an institution should be a professional manager and not a curator. These ideas are respectably held, for example, by many businessmen imbued with a sense that museums and their staff are not being handled professionally in financial, administrative and public relations terms. They argue that the average museum must be seen to function for education and entertainment. This phenomenon is encountered to a greater or lesser extent not only in Britain but throughout the developed world.

It is not my intention to pillory those who express such ideas, which are held in all sincerity and in a sense encapsulate some truth, even though it be out of date. I have already examined one element of this managerial idea in relation to the pressure exerted on the Museum to charge for entry, which I trust I have shown to be a false god. More serious is the idea that a museum is simply a business or a government department which can only be run on lines laid down by accountants, businessmen or civil servants. It seems quite incomprehensible that amateurs (for that is what such people are) should presume to instruct professionals on how they should manage their businesses. I would not advise Guinness, for example, how to make beer for profit on the basis of my museum experience, but many businessmen are only too keen to tell us how to run museums on the basis of their business experience. The English disease of the cult of the amateur raises its head here as in so many places. As taxpayers in a democratic country, we all have a right to criticise public institutions, but we also have a duty to listen to professionals' explanations.

A museum is not a business nor is it primarily a pedagogical institution, nor a part of the entertainment industry, although it is all these things in part. It is a complicated organism, and some of these complications have been explained in this book. Business experience, educational experience and showbiz experience all have their place in the running of a major museum: after all the Metropolitan Museum is said to be the fourth largest retailer in Manhattan, with a turnover in 1987/8 of $56.5m on its merchandising, affording a profit of $4.2m to the Museum; the museum school of the Boston Museum of Fine Arts had a budget in 1986 (the last available figures) of $5.5m, and in the British Museum the turnover on retail sales, merchandise and publishing was £3.8m in 1988/9. But the Museum must be run by people who are professionally involved in the collections and who are academically able to deal with them. Business ability, educational prowess and public relations experience must all be subordinated to this; all skills must be blended with sensitivity so that a team is created whose purpose is to protect the collections and present them to the public. The collections lie at the core of any museum's function; administrative ability is of course important in running a museum, but I believe that we have at the British Museum a good administrative team which can meld administration and collections into an efficient organisation. There are few museums in this country which do not have this combination of abilities.

It is the experience of all professionals in museums of art or cultural history that the public are interested in original objects in the permanent exhibitions, not in models, copies or dioramas. Many museums in Czechoslovakia, for example, (including the National Museum in Prague) experimented with permanent displays of copies – and were never visited. One of the least successful museums in Germany, from the point of view of the general public, is the Römisch-Germanisches Zentralmuseum in Mainz, in which practically every object is an electrotype or a cast; academics and teachers, however, use it with great enthusiasm. The great success of the Jorvik Viking centre in York is seen by many as evidence of the coming death of museums. Millions of visitors have enjoyed this experience, queueing in the rain for hours to experience a twenty-minute trip through a reconstructed Viking townscape. They enjoy their ride on an electric car and, passing quickly through a museum gallery (called in cowardly fashion 'artefact hall') emerge through a museum shop having had a cultural experience which can be matched nowhere else in Britain.

Although it has been tried elsewhere in Britain, there is no other successful similar experience: this is because the vast tourist reservoir of York has been skilfully tapped and a subject of enormous popular interest – the Vikings – has been glamourised and packaged by a successful marketing organisation. Interestingly, all the techniques used in this splendid show, save the electrical cars, have been used in the British Museum, even the smells, as anyone who saw the *Nomad and City* exhibition of 1976/8 will remember. But in this latter exhibition all the clothes and most of the objects were real and not reconstructions. There is an enormous capital investment in the Jorvik Centre: it must and will make a lot of money for the York Archaeological Trust, but it is not a museum, nor can it ever be one, in that it has no long-term responsibility, save as borrower of the objects in the 'artefact hall', for the objects it displays. It stands in the tradition of technological or industrial museums like that at Ironbridge in Shropshire, where the whole atmosphere of the industrial re-volution has been rescued and reconstructed in the manner of an ancient monument with no real collections, except for tools, moulds and certain products of the various workshops and factories. It is a brilliant reconstruction, but it is very different from a cultural-historical museum.

In one class of museum only is the curatorial function different – some of the major museums of natural history. Here the so-called curator is in reality a research worker pure and simple, and leaves the care and display of the collections to others, although even so the continual handling of the reserve collections is an essential part of the curatorial experience.

The future of the British Museum, however, depends on the display, conservation and curatorial care of its collections, under stringent academic control, in the age of an information explosion, when more and more data is demanded from the specialist. Managerial skills can and will be brought in. An academic must be found as Director who has the ability to administer the institution, and deal with its multifarious problems (and such characters are not such rare birds as certain non-professionals would suggest). This is what the Museum and its Trustees plan for the 1990s; it is an act of faith given the present climate of amateur managerial advice, but it is a valid and positive way of approaching our future. That there will be tensions is inevitable. The British Museum has seen it all before (it has even had one non-professional Director): there is no need to change something just because it has been in place for a long time, particularly if it is, as I believe the British Museum's organisation to be, efficient and reasonably successful.

Without belabouring our financial problems, I believe that politicians and others must recognise that museums add to the quality of life and that they should consequently fund us honestly and fully, even perhaps at times generously. I also believe that, although there is a tendency in this country towards charging for entry, this is swimming against the tide. Benefactors will, in the tradition of the nineteenth-century philanthropists, insist more and more on greater public access to institutions which are held in public trust. This is now becoming evident in America, where the élitism of certain institutions is challenging others to break the mould: the Minneapolis Institute of Arts, a considerable general arts museum, is being pressed by its local authority and some at least of its benefactors to extend free access from one evening a week to three days a week.

In one fashion Britain seems to be departing from the American experience, possibly, but by no means certainly, because of financial constraints. This is in the field of the 'blockbuster' exhibition. *Tutankhamun* was the first such exhibition in England in 1972/3. It resulted in queues round the Museum courtyard and building of a kind never seen before or since: 1.694 million visitors came to see it. Others that were also very successful included the

Turner Watercolours in 1975 and *The Vikings* in 1980, to name but two. The cost of mounting such major exhibitions is immense, approaching £1m at today's prices, a sum not easily obtainable. If the Museum could tempt half a million visitors at £2 per head it would be possible to cover such a cost, but unfortunately one cannot guarantee such figures. This is where sponsorship is useful. Sponsorship in its ideal form (in a Museum's view) means money on the table, but often all that is offered is a guarantee against loss, an occasionally acceptable, but awkward, relationship. There is, however, no doubt that in England (as in parts of the USA) the latter method is becoming less acceptable as the risk becomes greater. The former is the most sensible in that each side recognises its maximum commitment, but the latter appeals to the gambler.

It may well be that the appetite for special exhibitions in England is becoming jaded, or at least more selective. Exhibitions in London no longer achieve the great visitor numbers – half a million plus – that was once possible; perhaps the novelty has worn off. On the other hand, exhibitions tend to be seen (as is clear from surveys) by the more loyal viewer, by the older visitor who comes especially to the Museum for the purpose. Special exhibitions must clearly be continued, but they must be carefully controlled in terms of expenditure and subject. Even exhibitions of paintings on canvas (which are of course outside the interests of the British Museum) seem to be facing a decline in numbers. Special exhibitions will feature in our future programmes, but they can never provide a major source of income, nor be a primary *raison d'être* of the Museum.

One of the most important challenges facing the Museum must be the development of that portion of the Bloomsbury building shortly to be vacated by the British Library. The use of part of the vacated library space has itself been the subject of much political discussion since the announcement of the Library's move to St Pancras. The round Reading Room designed by Sydney Smirke to the requirements of Antonio Panizzi, the then Principal Librarian, and opened to the public in 1857, has a long and honourable history of service to scholars and politicians. Lenin, Marx and Sun yat-Sen used the room, as did great British thinkers and scholars; Shaw, Isaiah Berlin, Macaulay and others have drawn on its resources. It is one of the most famous rooms in

London, much visited as a shrine by politicians, particularly from socialist countries (its dome even appeared in the final scenes of the first English 'talkie', Hitchcock's *Blackmail*). There has been a considerable and somewhat sentimental campaign to retain it as the main reading room of the new Library. The impracticalities of this have been pointed out on many occasions: the problems of moving books to readers across a mile or more of busy London streets; the need to store books in modern conditions to arrest their deterioration, and the totally uneconomic situation whereby the British Library is at the moment struggling to exist in eighteen buildings in London. These, together with the advance of modern information technology, are only some of the arguments which can be advanced against the passionate pleas of the group of distinguished scholars who have led this campaign.

The decision of the British Library to abandon the Reading Room has now been upheld by Ministers. The British Museum has undertaken to preserve the room as a library and students' room. We hope to house the Department of Prints and Drawings there and to assist readers who use the Department of Ethnography's Library in the same place. We also hope that it will be possible to admit the public to a viewing area more easily so that this exciting room can be seen by as many people as possible.

The other great room which will be retained in its present form will be the King's Library. The fine royal bindings will disappear to St Pancras, but the shelves will continue to be filled with books. The rather haphazard display-cases at present detracting from the appearance of the room will be removed, and we shall introduce tactful vitrines in an attempt to create the atmosphere of a grand gentleman's library of the Georgian period. In them will be displayed *objets de vertu* – enamels, nielli, jewellery – to create as fitting an atmosphere as possible.

The preservation of these rooms will not be without its cost. First financial, for the two rooms have suffered from planning blight and were not redecorated and refurbished when they should have been. This maintenance will cost at least £4m, and it is now becoming a matter of urgency that provision should be made for these sums, or the rooms will deteriorate considerably. Second, in terms of architecture, some public rooms at present lined with book-cases will have to be adapted to the display of objects other than books. They must be allowed to be altered, otherwise they will fall into decay and we will not be able to use them. We expect problems with conservationist lobbies, but these problems must be overcome if we are to function properly as a museum.

Otherwise the future is full of possibilities. For the first time we shall be able to move the public round the building from north to south on ground-floor level. We shall have an adequate temporary exhibition space, possibly the present North Library, which can be permanently adapted for such purposes and allow a flexibility impossible at the moment in the constricted space of the New Wing Gallery. We shall be able to house our important archives in an honourable fashion and provide adequate office and library space for all the curatorial departments. We shall at last be able to provide an education centre in the main building.

Perhaps the most important potential development, however, is the possibility of returning the Department of Ethnography to the main building in Bloomsbury, away from the grand but totally unsuitable Museum of Mankind behind Piccadilly. The work of this Department and its collections depend on, and interlock with, those of other departments; the loss of day-to-day contact by the staff has slowed down the interactive serendipity which is at the base of all good museum work. The edges of the collections of all departments are blurred: European folk costume, for example, is housed in the Department of Ethnography, but Japanese kimonos are housed in the Department of Japanese Antiquities; non-native American graphic art is collected by the Department of Prints and Drawings, Inuit graphic art from Northern Canada by the Department of Ethnography. It is only through the close proximity of curators that collections may be used sensibly and this does not always happen at the moment. Furthermore, the daily contact of staff of different departments is one of the most excitingly stimulating elements in the life of a museum of this size; the present difficulty of contact between the two buildings particularly disadvantages the Department of Ethnography.

The public spaces which will be vacated by the departure of the Library will provide adequate room for the exhibition of our unique ethnographic collections. The physical nature of the material often means that this can only be shown for a short period. On the ground floor of the White Wing space is available (at present not open to the public) which should provide the flexibility required for temporary exhibitions of the high standard uniquely achieved at the Museum of Mankind. Similarly, some other areas can be made available to other departments starved of exhibition space, particularly the Departments of Prehistoric and Romano-British Antiquities, Medieval and Later Antiquities and Coins and Medals. We should be able to dedicate most of the King Edward vii Building to the collections of the Oriental departments, a process already started by the creation of the new Japanese and Islamic galleries and by the projected refurbishment of the Chinese and Indian collections.

The reserve collections of the Department of Ethnography are out-housed in East London. We must examine the possibility of moving them back to Bloomsbury, together with that section of the Department of Prehistoric and Romano-British Antiquities which deals with the Quaternary Period and the history of very early man. If we can move them, we must also move the section of the Department of Conservation which deals with organic materials – wood, feathers, basketry and so on – which is also housed there.

This done, the Museum can then be contained in only two buildings (for there is no intention of moving our collection of casts and the British archaeological archive from Olympia, where they are well housed and carefully looked after). This will enable the Museum to be run more efficiently, effectively and with a greater measure of control than at present. All the effort of the last few years in making the building sound, all the fund-raising and other efforts to refurbish our existing galleries by 1996 and the self-denial practised by the staff and curatorial departments in relation to their office accommodation, has been dedicated to this end. We are fulfilling one side of an implied bargain: we have resisted temptation to take on more and more outstations, to fill the remaining gaps on the site with large, new permanent buildings, so that the British Museum can be ready to step into a worthier mode of public display and public usage and into a leaner, more stimulating mode of scholarship.

All this will cost money; some of it must be public money. It is improbable, for example, that private cash will be forthcoming for the redecoration of the round Reading Room. It must be made politically possible for the British Museum to be treated as a special building which can be funded at a higher level for a few years in order that we may fulfil what is not a dream but a necessity. We could not and would not attempt to emulate the Grand Louvre project of the French with its public funding of 8 milliard francs; but government and public must realise that unless a comparatively modest amount of extra money is spent on the British Museum building at the stage when the British Library moves we shall be wasting a great national asset and failing to fulfil the obligation laid on the Trustees by our founding fathers when, at a meeting in the King's Arms Tavern on 15 March 1753, they resoundingly laid down the 'Fundamental Principles from which the Trustees do not think they can in Honor or Conscience depart':

> 1st. That the collection be preserved intire without the least diminution or separation.
> 2nd. That the same be kept for the use and benefit of the publick, who may have free access to view and peruse the same, at all stated and convenient seasons agreeably to the Will and intentions of the Testator, and under such restrictions as the Parliament shall think fit.

The Museum must continue to collect, to build on its present unique strengths and conserve its collections for the international community. Its staff are dedicated to this end, and to making the collections available to that audience. For this also we shall need honest funding and active political support. Through our experience and scholarship – and with the generosity of donors – we shall be able to keep acquiring objects for our collections. We cannot challenge the buying power of the handful of American museums of great wealth (the Metropolitan Museum of Art in New York spent nearly $16m on acquisitions during 1988; we spent about a sixth of that). We have a head start in that our holdings were already important and innovative before such museums were founded and, through scholarship, our staff have continued to lead the world in collecting.

The British Museum is confident that, with adequate funding, it can serve the international community, both through its collections and its sound learning, for ever.